THE ART OF PRACTICE

a self-help Guide for Music Students

Master the Basics

Master Yourself

Master your Instrument

HOWARD SNELL

Rakeway Music

© 2006 Howard Snell

First published 2006 ~ Pen Press
New Edition © 2011 ~ Rakeway Music
Third reprinting 2015 ~ Rakeway Music

The moral right of Howard Snell to be identified as the author of this work has been asserted by him in accordance with the Copyright, Designs and Patents Act 1988.

All rights reserved. No part of this publication
may be reproduced, stored in a retrieval system, or transmitted, in any form, or by any means, electronic, mechanical, photocopying, recording or otherwise, without the prior written permission of the publisher.

A Catalogue record for this book is available from the British Library.

ISBN 978-1-78003-843-8

Howard Snell Arts Ltd
99 Hampden Road
London NW8 0NU

www.rakewaymusic.com

Produced and distributed by:
Author Essentials
4 The Courtyard
South Street, Falmer
East Sussex BN1 9PQ

info@authoressentials.com
www.authoressentials.com

Dedication

To my wife, Angela

Acknowledgements

To **Margaret Veal, Jo Whiterod** and **Juliet Snell**
for their invaluable help, advice and criticism.

To **John White**
former Head of Strings at the Royal Academy of Music for quality of advice that cannot be bought.

Finally, my profoundest thanks go to my wife,

and again to **Angela**

both for buckets of encouragements
and always getting to the point fast.

All quotations are acknowledged in the text; everything else is my responsibility.

FOREWORD

During my early years as a student, the teaching I received was restricted to comments such as 'Do it like this' or more often 'Don't do that!' I heard very fine players do 'it' very well, but was given little real teaching guidance beyond 'Do that again' or 'Slower, please!' or 'I'll hear that again next week.'

What made players good or better or best was baffling. I was lucky as a child that a lot of performing experience came my way, not only on my own instrument but on the piano. I therefore had a decent foothold in the wider repertoire of music, not just that associated with the trumpet. I listened avidly to anything and everything on the radio from the symphonic repertoire across to big-band jazz. Equally important was my determination to learn at every opportunity.

When in the course of time I began to teach young people I did what I could in the usual way. However, midway through my working life I gave up my position as Principal Trumpet with the London Symphony Orchestra in order to conduct and subsequently to write music. I did decide however to continue as a teacher. The reason? I enjoyed it, and my students said that they valued what I did and how I did it.

It was then, as a non-player, that my approach to teaching quickly began to change: I began to focus totally on the student. I now recognised that the student's primary motivation must come from his or her own vision of performance, and not from mine. In short, the student must teach himself: I would prompt the vision and help in its discovery and development. I would be the remover of obstacles, the provider of supporting knowledge and their sources for both instrumental and musical matters, and above all a source of encouragement. I found myself devising both general and precise solutions – algorithms, patterns, routines, call them what you will – to general and precise problems, solutions that, as a young player, I would have died for. I also found that there was a very great deal of practice and performance wisdom buried deep, in fragments, in musical literature. I found my teaching work spreading into conducting, the writing of music, to musicians from all instruments and latterly The Art of Teaching.

I produced a book *The Trumpet, Its Practice and Performance, A Guide for Students* that contained what I had learned from conducting, listening, playing, teaching and observing how the best musicians think. Its reception by players and teachers alike was excellent, and included the comment, time after time, that what I had written applied to all instruments, even to actors and singers.

With the passage of time and further reflection this new book is the result. If it is of practical use to young, developing musicians I will be delighted. If it stimulates enjoyment of music beyond the locality of the individual's own instrument I will be even more pleased.

Some of the book will seem unorthodox, some of it may seem obscure on first reading – I have made very few concessions in the presentation of my ideas: I have never found that young people need patronising – but it gives as accurate a picture of my teaching of the skills of practice as I can.

INTRODUCTION

How to practise – how to manage it – how to manage oneself under pressure – musicians have been putting their minds to these matters since the beginning of musical time. Outstanding performers such as Bach (organ), Liszt and Chopin (piano), Paganini (violin), and Moyse (flute), took the crafts of practice, performance and innovation to new levels. A great deal is known about their methods and those of many others through their music, texts and first-hand reports of others. The process of creating new frontiers continues in brass and percussion, less so in wind, strings and keyboard.

Today the detailed skills of practice and learning are in danger of being swamped: in education the accent has swung so strongly to group work that much less time is available for individual practice. The ways of the past that created almost all of the greatest figures of music are becoming lost beneath these new social and educational attitudes. For the dedicated musician however, the true principles of solitary practice never change: they are timeless, are not subject to fashion and do not go out of date. Each generation must fully reclaim and revive the knowledge developed by previous generations. Once lost, it will be gone for ever.

This book attempts to restate these principles of practice and self-management. I have tried to avoid unnecessary complication and anything that smacks of 'psychology' either in a folksy or an academic form. Every procedure in the book has been tested hundreds of times. My approach concentrates on listening as the controller of practice and the engine of improvement. The instruction and descriptions are as near to 'read and do' as I can make them, and need no extra words to make them work. However I always explain my background thinking.

All young animals play in order to learn. As children we are able to start to play music when we have amassed enough knowledge of nature and of ourselves. However important music becomes to us when adults, the elements of play and enjoyment must remain central to our performance and practise of music.

USING THE BOOK

The book is in two parts, CLEARING THE GROUND and PRACTICE, and is not designed as a front-to-back read-through book. These parts are then divided into chapters that can either be read and referred to singly, or read through as a set of linked ideas about practice and performance. Because each chapter is meant to be self-sufficient and able to be read on its own, there are repetitions of both wordings and of thoughts in the text. Rather than including an index I have collated fuller headings in the contents section for better reference. Music is not really divisible into separate topics, but in order to gain entry and write about it, doors have to be created in the walls. However the doors all lead back into the original single space, the playing of music.

Part One – CLEARING THE GROUND – deals firstly with the foundations of music performance, then with the foreground skills with which performance is built. Part Two – PRACTICE – discusses both the planning of practice and specific problem-solving techniques. The music examples are pointers to illustrate the technique being discussed: instances that most suit a specific instrument must be found in the repertoire of that instrument. Where I have gone into more detail I have used the piano repertoire as being the instrument most common to all musicians. Again, the principles involved can be transferred to the reader's own instrument.

For those who are sensitive to these things please forgive the exclusive use of 'he' and its derivatives: clumsy tripping over endless 'he or she'-zes breaks the flow too much for my ear and eye. I have followed the English spellings for 'practice' as a noun and 'practise' when a verb. The text boxes contain quotations, anecdotes and a mixture of personal points that are intended to add flavour and colour, but are not part of the essential argument.

CONTENTS

FOREWORD	1
INTRODUCTION	3
USING THE BOOK	5

PART ONE: CLEARING THE GROUND
The Foundation

SOUND	15
What is our musical sound?	15
Personal sound	15
Impersonal sound	15
LISTENING	16
How audiences and musicians listen differently	16
Listening actively	16
Listening passively	16
Different types of listening for practising and performing	16
Creative listening	17
LEARNING MUSIC	18
What is learning?	18
Learning quickly	18
Learning thoroughly	19
General comments	19
READING MUSIC	21
Reading described	21
Good reading helps good playing	21
Achieving the standard	22
Sight reading: a crash course	22
Improving further	23
The eye learns to hear and the ear learns to see	24
AWARENESS, ATTENTION AND CONCENTRATION	25
What are they?	25
Awareness described	25
Attention described	25
Concentration described	25
Awareness in practice and performance	26
Why are some people unaware?	26
Key points	26
Awareness: a player's best friend	27
MEMORISATION	28
What is memory?	28
The different types	28
The stages in memorisation	28
The value of memory in solo performance	29
How to get more from your memory: 1 & 2	29

The Foreground

TIME & RHYTHM — 33
    What are they? The same? Different? — 33
    Time and timing — 33
    Rhythm — 33
    The hidden importance of time and timing — 33
    Rhythm in action — 33
    Time and rhythm: related matters — 34
    Further tempo matters — 35
    Pulse time versus mechanical time — 37
    If you are what you eat... — 37

TIME PATTERNS — 38

MELODY PLAYING, PHRASING & ARTICULATION — 43
    The nature of melody, phrasing, articulation etc. — 43
    Achieving a good melodic line — 45
    A simple exercise — 46

ARTICULATION (or The Presentation of Detail) — 48
    Types — 48
    Starts, Stops and Shapes — 48
    Achieving different articulations — 48
    Articulation, tempo and technique — 49

DYNAMICS — 50
    General issues — 50
    Specific issues — 50
    Developing soft dynamics — 50
    Developing loud dynamics — 51
    Developing dynamic control — 51
    Approaching individual works — 51
    Establishing levels — 51
    Why are dynamics so important? — 52
    Dynamics and balance — 52

INTONATION — 53
    What's the Problem? — 53
    What is 'natural tuning'? — 53
    'Equal temperament'? — 53
    Why the conflicts? — 54
    Melodic issues — 54
    Harmonic issues — 54
    General matters — 55
    Tuning groups of instruments — 56

NTERPRETATION: 1 — 58
    Interpretation defined — 58
    The tools to use — 58
    Other people's ideas: compare and contrast — 59
    The treatment of detail — 59
    Individuality! Who needs it? — 60

NTERPRETATION: 2	61
Building a framework for interpreting music	61
The stages	61
Serious practice	64
Living with success	65

PART TWO: PRACTICE

Chapter 1: ASSEMBLING THE TOOLBOX	69
The five compartments of the toolbox	69
1. Managing yourself and your practice (Chapter 2)	69
2. Practice: using the musical elements (Chapters 3 – 6)	69
3. Practice: using alteration, distortion & simplification (Chapters 7 – 14)	69
4. Mental skills (Chapters 15 – 17)	69
5. Looking after yourself (Chapters 18 – 21)	70
Practice techniques: the key	70
Chapter 2: MANAGING YOUR PRACTICE	71
The expertise of practising	71
Preparing for practice	71
Practising	72
General points	73
Aims, goals and making progress	75
Expertise and know-how	76
Chapter 3: Using the Elements ~ TURNING SOUND INTO TONE	77
Making the sound	77
Sound into tone	77
Chapter 4: Using the Elements ~ CREATING THE LINE	79
The foundation of the line	79
Producing *legato*	79
Producing *staccato*	79
Compare and contrast	79
Summary	81
Chapter 5: Using the Elements ~ MANIPULATING THE ELEMENTS	83
The three elements	83
Examples	84
Chapter 6: Using the Elements ~ LOOPS	86
What is a 'loop'?	86
What does it do?	86
How does it work?	86
Using it	86
Summary	88
Chapter 7: Alteration, Distortion & Simplification ~ SLURRINGS & THEIR USES	89
Underlying principles	89
Using Slurring as a control	89

Chapter 8: Alteration, Distortion & Simplification ~
   ALTERATION & DISTORTION   90
   Tempo alteration   90
   The benefits of variable tempo practice   90
   How does it work?   90
   Facing a problem passage   91
   Solutions   91
   So what was the problem?   92

Chapter 9: Alteration, Distortion & Simplification ~
   TARGET NOTES & ANCHOR NOTES   93
   Target Notes   93
   Anchor Notes   93
   Poise and composure   95
   Footnote: Bach and Sons   95

Chapter 10: Alteration, Distortion & Simplification ~ TRANSPOSITION   96
   Why transpose?   96
   How does transposition improve things?   96

Chapter 11: Alteration, Distortion & Simplification ~
   SIMPLIFICATION & ANALYSIS   97
   Why simplify?   97
   How does it work?   97

Chapter 12: Alteration, Distortion & Simplification ~
   SCALES & ARPEGGIOS   99
   What are they?   99
   What is so good about them?   99
   Creating fluency and confidence   99
   What do they do apart from annoy and bore?   100
   How Scales and Arpeggios help problem solving   100
   Organising them painlessly   101
   Practising them intelligently   101
   Further guidance   102

Chapter 13: Alteration, Distortion & Simplification ~
   SCALES & ARPEGGIO EXAMPLES   103

Chapter 14: Mind Skills ~ THE INNER EAR ~ AURALISATION   109
   What is the inner ear? and Auralisation?   109
   What are the uses of the inner ear (Auralisation)?   109
   Some general points   110

Chapter 15: Mind Skills ~ THE INNER EYE ~ VISUALISATION   111
   What is the inner eye? and Visualisation?   111
   What are the uses of the inner eye (Visualisation)?   111

Chapter 16: Mind Skills ~ THE INNER VOICE ~ VOCALISATION   113
   What is the inner voice? and Vocalisation?   113
   What are the uses of Vocalisation?   113
   Hands & voice   113
   Mime   113

Chapter 17: Looking After Yourself ~ ANXIETY CONTROL	115
What is anxiety?	115
What else causes anxiety?	115
What are the effects of anxiety?	115
Controlling anxiety	115
What are the build-ups to performance anxiety?	116
Controlling anxiety in the short term	116
Exercises	116
Anxiety control on a performance day	117
Controlling anxiety long term	117
Conclusion	118
Drugs for 'nerves'?	118
Chapter 18: Looking After Yourself ~ POSTURE	120
The value of good posture	120
Achieving it	120
When we were babies…	121
Now we are old(er)…	121
Chapter 19: Looking After Yourself ~ PHYSICAL CONDITIONING	122
What has physical conditioning to do with musicians?	122
Exercise	122
Diet	122
Chapter 20: Looking After Yourself ~ HOW TO BE A GOOD STUDENT	124
Choosing a teacher	124
The student at college	124
Choosing to be a good student	125
What comes next?	125
Self-development versus standardisation	126
Self-development and the computer	126
Chapter 21: Endnote 1 ~ PERFORMANCE	128
Why is performance different to practice?	128
The musician as performer	128
The audience-eye view of a performance	128
Performance skills	129
Preparation for a solo performance	131
The degree recital	131
In the orchestra	133
Compare and contrast popular music performance	133
Chapter 22: Endnote 2 ~ PRACTICE SUMMARY	134
Chapter 23: Endnote 3 ~ PRACTICE CHECK LIST	135

Part One

CLEARING THE GROUND

The Foundation

SOUND

What is our musical sound?

Our musical sound is our musical fingerprint. It identifies us and we identify with it. Is this why it often seems that the instrument chooses us? The main reason that most people take up an instrument is its sound, its personality, the noise it makes, the feel of it, the sympathy of its vibration. Why else would anyone want to carry around a large lump like a tuba or a string bass?

A good sound combines both warmth and brilliance. An expert teacher can 'read' a sound and diagnose a player's technical problems from it, in the same way that a doctor reads our symptoms with a stethoscope. Sound is not simply what we hear or play, but equally a feeling in the body: it is a special harmony of sensation between sound and feeling and is one of the core satisfactions about performing and listening to music.

For the performer, fine sound quality enhances confidence, because it is both deeply satisfying and encouraging. Improvement in sound quality lifts all other aspects of playing, as a rising tide lifts all boats. Try to avoid an obsession with technique and safety, because they elbow out your attention to sound, and by themselves cause worry and loss of confidence. Once these anxieties grip a player, sound quality deteriorates. Keep beauty of sound at the front of your musical picture.

Personal sound

Whether the performer intends to produce a brilliant, a sweet or a sonorous effect, the underlying sound must be pure. A sound is pure when it is produced without excess effort. We must measure effort by what is needed, and not exert impatient force or false bravura to try to conquer a problem. Purity of sound always captivates the listener.

Impersonal sound

An obsession with technique and safety tends to produce a sound that has no personality, with an off-the-shelf standardised quality like a mass-produced object. The character of an industrial product however cleverly made may be efficient but it will always be without character and without any flexibility of expression. For a player with serious musical ambitions, individual personality of sound is vital.

LISTENING

How audiences and musicians listen differently

Audience members listen to music as a total experience, rarely noticing a player's technique unless it is special. We musicians listen to music in the same general way, but we analyse how the performance is created at the same time as enjoying the experience of listening.

Expert musicians listen to the detail of music and performance very precisely: the purpose being to use the resulting information to become better performers. The exercises, loops and patterns given in this book achieve their results by concentrating players' listening on the precise problem moments. As soon as effective listening takes place, the ear identifies what needs to be done and guides the technique's search for a solution.

Listening actively

The quality of a player's listening determines his quality of performance. Serious music requires active, concentrated listening for musicians and non-musicians alike. Only when listening is intense and sustained does understanding of what we are doing become clear.

Listening passively

If it is true that we are what we eat, we musicians are what we hear. Today, with background music everywhere, we are in danger of becoming de-sensitised – to sound, to volume, to taste, to stimuli of all kinds. The presence of such a huge volume of ambient music represents a real danger for musicians – because it is musically meaningless. Silence was the background against which all the great composers worked. Silence, not noise, should also be the background for the work of players. Listen passively as little as possible. Above all, never play or practise passively.

Different types of listening for practising and performing

Practising and performing require two different types of listening. While practising, the expert player listens to his own work, then compares it to his ideal mental image. He then alters the actual to bring it closer to the ideal.

Other musicians' performances allow us to build up a musical picture of what is possible and so we develop better possibilities ourselves. While performing, a musician must listen to the other players as closely as he does to himself. Quality of ensemble depends on players' listening to each other, which then creates musical rapport. Practice is undertaken alone, but almost all music performance is a social activity, with others.

The quality of ensemble that results from good listening is superior to that which results from visual clues such as time-beating from a conductor's baton, or verbal rehearsal instructions. When every member of an ensemble is feeling and listening to the music, a natural togetherness is the result, well beyond that which can be initiated by a run-of-the-mill conductor.

Creative listening

The range of styles required of the modern player is wider than ever before. These can only be learnt by listening expertly, then imitating what has been heard. The ear can target specific sounds or it can listen wide-screen: it moves around the sonic spectrum as fast as the eye does in the visual sphere.

All chamber music performance – without conductor and in small groups – requires the highest quality of active listening. It is not only an essential part of training for all student musicians, but an experience of continuing value to every performer, of whatever level of achievement. Take every opportunity to perform in small groups.

To an expert ensemble, the time-beating element of a conductor's work is largely irrelevant: good players rarely pay close attention to that aspect of a conductor's work. Setting tempi, handling changes of tempi and the use of gesture to indicate feeling and the progress of the music, these are the only - and very occasional - signs that players need in order to supplement their listening.

The conductor's function can be positive if he is able to provide a stimulating and unifying framework for the players.

The customary orchestral musician's reply when asked, "Who was conducting?" is "Sorry, I didn't look." He may not have looked but he would have been aware of what he needed, and whether it was delivered from the podium.

LEARNING MUSIC

What is learning?

Learning is the acquisition of knowledge. The knowledge of a piece of music is created through a number of different learning processes, some physical, some intellectual. A musical work that has been well-learned can be refreshed and performed within hours, even after a long break.

Learning quickly

Imagine the following scenario: you are a young player who has been asked to perform an unknown work at one week's notice. Result? Excitement and uncertainty. Can you do it? The piece is difficult but not impossible. The fee is not good. Forget the fee: for a young musician that is never important. Accept the offer!

- Establish a calm attitude to the task. The picture will then become clearer and the outline of what has to be done will emerge.
- Glance through the piece, establish the whole picture without fussing about detail.
- Expect to read fast. The professional expects to read fast, accurately, and to play in the appropriate style within a couple of read-throughs at most. This expectation starts up the reading process with the right amount of urgency, generating speed of thought and sharpness of judgement.
- Consciously recognise the composer's patterns of writing. Unless it is a radical new work there will not be a great deal in an unknown piece that you will not have seen before. This is where your general knowledge, experience and previous study of repertoire will be invaluable.

> *If, on the brink of the performance, there are still one or two problems not totally solved, two courses remain. Take a chance. Trust yourself to find the extra. The best players are lifted by these tests.*
>
> *As a fallback position prepare very slight changes to the 'impossible' moments, opt-outs to be used in emergency – a change of note in a fast passage, a note left out: in other words, professional tactics.*

- First impressions as to how to shape the music must become firm without delay. Relate the work to others of the same type. Use of the techniques suggested in the chapters on Interpretation will speed up effective learning.
- Whether you intend to play with or without the score it is vital to commit as much as possible to memory, especially the awkward corners. Have you already developed the ability to memorise fast and recall accurately?

- As soon as possible play through the music without interruption, in complete sections. Much of it will fall into place quickly, thus isolating the passages of critical difficulty. The inefficient learner fiddles with the details while Rome burns.
- Do not waste time playing passages that are well within your grasp. Focus on the difficult moments and mobilise every possible practice technique. In the second part of the book there are enough practice techniques to solve most problems. Be imaginative. Create new ones if necessary.
- Finally you must remember that it is a performance, not a play-through. Whatever misgivings and insecurities lie under the surface, you, the performer, must carry off the event with panache and apparent confidence. The swan may be paddling furiously under the water, but the onlooker must see only the calm gliding effect.

Having read the above, are you in good enough shape to take that special chance when it comes? Be ready, now, before it comes.

Learning thoroughly

- Expect to learn the basics of a major work quickly. Regard one week as ample. Otherwise put the work away till you are nearer the level necessary.
- Work on it for a while, then rest it for a while. Return to it later, then rest it again – and so on until the piece is totally secure. Rest periods are essential: they allow the sub-conscious mind to sort and absorb the material that has been practised.

> *When learning a new work, do not listen to any recordings until your own performance is thoroughly settled. Develop your own musical mind: if you copy others and don't exercise your own judgement, you will not grow as a musician.*

During my time as Principal Trumpet with the London Symphony Orchestra, without fail I would keep an eye on the schedule some six months ahead, noting the pieces which I didn't know or hadn't played for some years. If necessary I would put in a few days' work – six months ahead – on the most difficult passages, and then forget them until the concert rehearsals. What I learned early in my career was that my sub-conscious mind, if I give it time and leave it alone, absorbs material and organises it ready for performance – by itself. Prepare – rest – succeed.

General comments

We learn well and quickly when we are interested in something. The initial excitement that launches us into playing an instrument can disappear very quickly. That is why it is necessary for a talented child to adopt, from the start, a stable pattern of work: when the initial excitement of playing starts to evaporate, good habits are needed to sustain the learning process.

Today, in many educational circles, there is an antagonism to learning. Learning must be fun, we are told, without reference to the deliberate effort that must go into the acquiring of knowledge. We all need fun at the appropriate time, but equally we need deep satisfaction in real achievement. In music, lack of knowledge shows up in poor performance.

Strangely, even in subjects that interest us, we remember certain things easily, while others, to begin with, simply will not stick. In these cases there is no alternative to hard work, repeating the material time and time again until it does at last stick in the mind. Once information or knowledge is firmly remembered it can then be gradually absorbed and used naturally. This is not a fun process, and anyone who tells you that learning should be easy is not telling the truth.

On entry into the higher levels of education, a student is largely left alone, and is assumed to be competent at learning, having got thus far on the education ladder. Nothing is further from the truth. Most students have no plan, no strategy, no idea. 'How-to-learn', the key skill for any student, is never covered as a topic in itself. The assumption is made both in school and college that the student will, somehow, just learn.

An appetite and skill for learning leads to enjoyment of both one's work and one's life. Effective use of memory enables fulfilment of aims and goals: the better it works, the deeper the fulfilment. Is that important? The Ancient Greeks regarded Memory as the Mother of all the other Muses. She still is.

READING MUSIC

"Reading is to the mind what exercise is to the body."
                                                    Richard Steele

Reading described

Reading is a learned skill. The eye sees the symbols, then the brain remembers, recognises and interprets them. Repetition speeds the progress, but exceptional speed is secured only by conscious effort. To improve beyond the comfort zone, deliberately adopt the best techniques in order to achieve greater speed and comprehension.

When I encounter a student whose reading is slow and inaccurate, the conversation usually goes like this:

'Can you read music as easily as you read a newspaper?'

'No.'

'Why not? Do you seriously want to become a professional musician? Or is someone going to pay you to read newspapers?'

Reading music as if it were words is the standard for professionals, every day of their lives. The ability to read music instantly is one of the basics of professionalism.

Good reading helps good playing

The reading of music happens the instant before playing, just when the preparation to play is entering its critical phase. If that moment of reading is confused and uncertain, the physical act of playing will be badly affected. If the eye and brain are incapable of recognising and sorting the written symbols quickly and accurately, the brain will be unable to send confident and positive instructions to the body about what to play. The 'how' to play, the feeling of the music, the real purpose of the music, will be left unattended. Upgrade the speed and accuracy of reading skills and immediately you will experience the significantly beneficial effect on playing skills. Good reading creates space and time, and therefore a comfortable relationship with the instrument.

Think of sportsmen. The best are both sure and unhurried. They read their game with mental time to spare, therefore their physical movements are to the point, economical in effort and precise in output. They are very intelligent in terms of their game, whatever one might think of some of them outside their sport. The poor sportsman is all arms and legs, uncoordinated, late and slow with responses and moves. Similarly, a poor music reader is always fumbling for the next solution, deaf to ensemble matters, intonation etc., in a desperate hurry to find the next note before it is too late. Speed and certainty are essential to any competent physical action, whether walking, jumping, playing, or any other complex skill. Poor reading is a significant cause of poor performance and is one of the main barriers to playing progress.

Achieving the standard

At the highest level of professional playing, in situations when time is money, reading sharpens very fast, or professionally you 'die'. The player with ambition must therefore have top quality reading ready for one of those few opportunities. (It may be tomorrow!) It is not good enough to wait until the chances appear and then learn to read well afterwards. Many students wake up to this matter too late. The conversation with the teacher usually runs as follows:

'What can I do about my sight-reading, it's terrible?'

'Have you followed my advice and practised sight-reading daily?'

'Er, no!'

End of conversation.

Sight reading: a crash course

Take four fifteen-minute periods per day. Read through previously unseen, unknown material, with the metronome set at the correct speeds. The aim is to make the eye and the brain work faster. Speed reading forces the eye and mind to work faster, so treat the eye/brain as lazy muscles to be exercised vigorously. You will feel very tired: brain work uses more energy than body work.

- The first and absolute priority is to read the rhythms correctly. The pitches will largely look after themselves.
- Do not stop in the course of a passage for any reason whatsoever, except a death in the family.
- Don't think or interfere, just do it!

> One of the great educational values of music is that it develops processes of thinking in general, and in particular the ability to link physical action to intellectual understanding. As a child, in classes of forty or fifty (and sometimes more), I can remember taking part in singing classes, all children having been taught simple tonic-solfa music reading. The processes of personal intellectual activity, (reading and understanding), personal physical activity, (singing), in a co-operative social context (with others), are of the greatest value. The fact that the majority of those in the classes would not have had any further direct contact with music performance is irrelevant: the capability for flexible intelligence created by this apparently simple activity, serves in innumerable non-musical contexts. It is tragic, for the continuation of musical civilisation, that very few schools today promote the necessary discipline to hold classes of that kind. Official educational opinion is unable to recognise the need for young minds to be trained in this way.

- Expect to read well; there will be nothing on the page you haven't seen before.
- The reading material can be anything. Tidiness and quality of performance are of no importance whatsoever.
- Look back after a week and you will see an enormous difference. Continue this way until you feel thoroughly in charge.

Improving further

Read the music in chunks

Seeing can be improved. The eye moves in stops and starts, not smoothly: it can make up to four focussing stops per second. At each stop, the eye 'photos' a small chunk of information, which is passed to the brain. Because of the time lapse involved between the sending and the processing of the information, the eye is able to move on to the next chunk. The good reader takes in chunks or groups of notes whereas the poor reader takes in isolated symbols one at a time. Consciously take in larger and larger groups.

Control the speed and type of eye movement

Use a slightly slower, smoother eye movement. Avoid the temptation to check back on material already passed. Speed of reading will improve thereafter. 'Sweep' the page with more open (peripheral) vision. Avoid peering, and leaning forward anxiously when reading and playing.

Find the patterns

The ability to recognise patterns instantly, without any pause for conscious thought, is the key to the effective reading of music, because composers combine these patterns in varying ways. But beware sequences of a pattern! In the music of good composers patterns and sequences of patterns are usually changed just when you expect them to continue.

Read without playing

The habit of reading music scores away from the instrument has untold benefits. Not only is reading improved, but so is interpretative ability, by being freed from the instrument.

Snapshot memorisation

Make a habit of snapshot memorisation of passages such as (1) the start of pieces, (2) new tempi, (3) difficult accelerandi and ritardandi, and (4) awkward corners where full attention is needed for the ensemble. This habit leads to significant improvement in solo and ensemble performance. The only difficulty is to start doing it. Good examples for strings are as follows:

Example 1 Mozart: Eine Kleine Nachtsmusik

Example 2 Beethoven: Fifth Symphony, 1st Mvt.

Avoid tunnel-vision reading – where you are unaware of your musical surroundings – at all costs. Be aware of the world beyond yourself.

The eye learns to hear and the ear learns to see

In common with all co-operation between different senses, the separate parts must function well in isolation, before being combined. The eye intakes most of our everyday information. Link it to the ear to develop your skills, by imagining the sounds of the written score. If you can hear a C major chord when you see it on the score, you can go on from there.

Similarly when you hear music, envisage how it is written ... yes, in detail!

*When asked whether he could hear, in his mind, a score as complex as **Till Eulenspiegel**, the conductor George Szell ... always a man for the acid home truth ... replied, 'What do you take me for? An amateur?'*

AWARENESS, ATTENTION & CONCENTRATION

What are they?

They are the different ways we apply our mental energy.

Awareness described

Watchfulness, being on one's guard, being aware (be-ware!), are all definitions of awareness, and suggest the workings of the mind when a general sense of danger is present. All performers must be aware of the whole musical space in which a performance takes place, alert to everything, whether playing in a duo, a small ensemble or a full orchestra. It is easy to be aware of what is happening around us while we are doing nothing ourselves, but during playing it is harder to keep this whole picture in view. A defining characteristic of the expert musician is that he remains constantly aware of what is going on even while playing.

> *As mentioned earlier, effort drives out skill. In order not to try too hard with the effort of concentration, expert performers are always careful to stay at about 80% to 90% during performance, not pushing up against the limit. This is the point at which the finest performances occur. Descriptions of peak performances in sport are always described as having happened easily, in a flowing manner, almost without effort.*

Attention described

'Pay attention!' This comment has been directed at all of us at some time! Attention directs the mind, seriously, towards a subject. In the case of the musician, the focus of attention is our personal performance. Improvement requires steady, active application of mental energy.

Concentration described

Concentration is the most intense kind of attention. At its height it is completely self-contained and self-containing. If too much effort is used, concentration becomes too strained, too rigid, everything else is blotted out, and awareness is lost. With too much effort, performance quality tails off, as can be seen when sportsmen try too hard.

Awareness in practice and performance

All of our senses can be directed at precise targets. For example, focusing sight upon a specific object is the easiest example to imagine. Our sense of hearing works in the same way. When a player practises alone, the senses are focussed inwardly on self-improvement. Playing in public can feel so different, strange and threatening because it is necessary for the performer to focus outwards for a single once-only effort.

The degree to which a player must be aware, varies constantly according to the musical demands of the situation. The ability to remain sensitive to the changing picture of a performance is one major sign of a master performer. Without this kind of situation-intelligence, it is impossible to respond and link up with fellow performers. The musical side of awareness is the ability to listen while playing, which is a vital element in musicianship. The very act of aware listening triggers musical rapport automatically.

Why are some people unaware?

Why should someone who has chosen to be a musician have a problem with awareness? Why should awareness and attention wander? Lack of awareness suggests a mixture of disinterest, boredom and worry, a sure pointer to poor work. The player who regularly arrives late at rehearsals or lessons, yawning and unprepared, is certainly not going to make a career. The musician who is bored during practice or rehearsal, and pays no attention, will suddenly become alarmed and anxious during a performance, when the danger inherent in all performance rushes to the fore. The truth will dawn: he doesn't know what is going on! Attention, awareness and concentration must be activated every day: the player with a professional attitude works well in all situations, not just the 'interesting' ones. It is easy to be interested in exciting new situations, but that is for the person who plays only for fun.

> *Number one rule of survival – never be the weakest member of an ensemble: you will not last long. If you are the second weakest you may have a little time! Jungle rules apply!*

Key points

'Interest', 'Method' and 'Professionalism' are the keys. Awareness is always alive and present when interest is there. Like all skills, it is born of patient, methodical habits. The student must cultivate professional-level awareness, attention and concentration as the foundation to playing. Empty heads are bored, and it is the bored who are unaware.

What is needed is a plan of work, with constant variation, rest and relaxation in good proportions, plus clear aims and goals. Enjoyment then flourishes and will make sure that attention, awareness and concentration are in full control.

Awareness: a player's best friend

One story about the height of musical awareness concerns Otto Klemperer and the Philharmonia Orchestra, during that conductor's last years. He was certainly a great conductor, in spite of suffering crippling illness towards the end of his life. He managed to continue working, achieving some magnificent performances by sheer strength of will and personality.

At a recording session of a late Bruckner Symphony, the slow movement was greeted by the producer as being wonderful beyond belief. In fact an extremely ill Klemperer, conducting seated, had fallen asleep just after the start of the twenty-minute movement. The orchestra completed the movement perfectly on their own, their awareness and musicianship needing only minimal visual contact between the leader, the principals and the rest of the orchestra.

> *At the other extreme comes a memory of an educational concert, given many years ago, on the subject of what a conductor actually does. I suggested that we played the final section of **Stravinsky's The Rite of Spring** by ourselves, something we did at concerts quite regularly, in the face of the speculative flailings of some stars of the podium. A look of horror crossed the face of this particular maestro. 'Oh no! That would really give the game away!' he said.*

MEMORISATION

What is memory?

Memory is what we know. Without memory we can do nothing and are nobody. We learn natural physical actions during early childhood, such as walking. Intellectual memory we develop methodically, whether for arithmetic or music performance. Playing from memory brings many benefits to the performer and to the audience. All that is needed is the will, backed up by patient application of simple methods.

The different types

First – **See-and-Forget Memory** is used for short term playing. Commercial sessions and freelance work require this skill to a high degree, with extreme speed and efficiency in problem solving. There is an even shorter version that I call **Snapshot Memory**, mentioned earlier in the chapter on Reading Music

Second – **Working Memory** is used for learned, but un-memorised repertoire. It is prompted by the music page. Normal orchestral reading (re-reading) of known repertoire is in this category.

Third – **Permanent Memorisation** needs only occasional refreshment.

The stages in memorisation

1. Inputting

Learning a piece of music, so that it is known well enough to be read with ease, involves passing it through short-term memory enough times for it to be firmly held in medium-term, or working memory. Speed up the process by making a conscious effort to remember while reading, as one does travelling along unfamiliar roads for the first time, knowing that the journey has to be made again.

> *The true art of memory is the art of attention.*
>
> Dr Johnson

As soon as a piece is thoroughly known, test yourself to find out what has been memorised so far. You will recall a surprising amount, but do not be discouraged by the passages which have not stuck automatically: there is a seeming randomness about what sticks in the memory and what doesn't, which can disconcert and upset. The answer lies in frequent brief repetitions. Remain unemotional about failures along the way. How many repetitions? As many as it takes! If you persist when a problem seems insoluble, the next moment sees a glimpse of light. Keep trying.

Next, memorise each passage consciously. Back them up by taking a snapshot of each passage as a picture: visualise it and read. This latter ability varies from person to person but develops with regular use, as do most faculties! If a player can memorise an ordinary melody then a Concerto presents no problem: the latter just needs more work than the former.

2. Retaining

Strengthen the recall of memorised music by repeatedly running the music through in the mind. Take care not to memorise in any errors. Consolidate memory of a piece of music by working without the instrument. In this situation try out different approaches, tempi, phrasings and nuances. (See the chapters on Mind Skills in Part Two.)

With repertoire already brought to performance level in the past, revise regularly for memorisation. You will also notice a maturing of interpretation.

3. Recalling

Before playing, freshen the memory by reading the score silently. Clean up the memory by checking, especially the main direction changes in the music, and other points of uncertainty. If this simple process is undertaken thoroughly, problems will not arise.

The value of memory in solo performance (Would an actor appear on stage to play Hamlet with the script in hand?)

Memorisation demands a deep knowledge of the music. It allows interaction with both the music and the audience, freeing the performer from the printed page. With the removal of the page, the performer can attend to the real business in hand: expressing the music to the listener. The printed page and the music-stand otherwise are likely to act as a barrier to the audience: as if the performer is only allowing the audience to overhear a private read-through.

Playing from secure memory creates confidence that spreads to both the expressive and technical qualities of the playing. Close reading under pressure inevitably creates tightness of breathing. (For a discussion of this subject see the chapter on Anxiety Control.) While playing without music, the performer can look around the concert hall, with relaxed posture, breathing and vision.

How to get more from your memory: 1

Initially, spend a short period consciously memorising – say ten or fifteen minutes.

Then take a ten-minute break.

Revise the memorised material without the printed page.

Take an hour's break.

Make a final review of the material.

The next day repeat, until mastered.

How to get more from your memory: 2

> Sing or vocalise passages. Memory benefits greatly from this.
>
> Memorise accompaniments. Identify and remember special cues, writing them in the part.
>
> In tacet passages that are confusing, back-up the memory by consciously remembering bars rest as a sequence of numbers e.g. 24 plus 5 plus 6.
>
> With moments that won't stay in the memory, transpose them into a number of keys. This helps to fix them.
>
> Write out those final few moments that refuse to stick in the mind.
>
> First Steps. When taking the first steps do not be discouraged by failure: build up your own mixture of techniques.

Remembering to use one's memory may seem like a joke, but failing to remember is the primary reason for most performers' poor practising habits. Write down practice schedules and points of interest that come up in lessons! Inefficient practising leads to slow or stalled progress, not just in memory playing, but on all fronts. Check the timetables I give in the 'Managing your practice' Chapter in Part Two, for your use of time and your work-in-progress. Reduce the potential damage which poor memory can inflict.

Four Ways

1. Music and Instrument
2. Music alone
3. Instrument alone
4. In the Mind – no Music, no Instrument

Acquire memory-recall under pressure. It is one of the most valuable life skills. Exercise your memory while distractions are present. It isn't easy and to start it may worry or annoy, but it is good for you, both as a musician and as a person. Memory is all you have ... and all you are!

CLEARING THE GROUND

The Foreground

TIME & RHYTHM

What are they? The same? Different?

Some musicians talk about time and rhythm very sloppily, as if they are same thing. They are not. We need some definitions.

Time and timing

Time is exactness by the clock, the 'when' of playing. Timing is the ability to place the starts of notes exactly where the time requires them.

Rhythm

Rhythm is the 'how' of playing the time. Rhythm is shown by the notes being subtly played louder and softer, as, for example, in the relationship between the downbeat and the other beats in a bar. Rhythm creates *metre*: bar lengths in twos, threes and their multiples. Hand in hand with pitch and with expression (detailing), rhythm is a primary creator of phrasing.

The hidden importance of time and timing

As mentioned in the previous paragraph, playing any instrument requires the co-ordination of a number of physical actions. These faculties must work together at the *same instant*, in spite of the fact that each of these actions – bow/tongue/arm, fingers etc. – has its own different speed of response. Any group of notes will place different levels of demand upon each of these technical elements. The certainty and precision of this co-operation determines whether one's overall technique is secure or not. Without precision in timing, our physical actions will not co-ordinate.

The underlying aim of the practice options, given in the 'Toolbox' chapters, is to create certainty through the development of high-quality listening. Effective listening co-ordinates these faculties and issues orders that the body tries to obey. I understand that this may be an unusual way of describing the road to technical improvement, but good listening is always the first step in the process that creates technique and capability.

Rhythm in action

In the examples, a crotchet (quarter note) is divided into three semiquavers (sixteenths) and a semiquaver rest. This group is shown in four different time contexts. The rhythmic identities are created by varying the accents.

In the first three examples *(Examples 3, 4, 5)* the first bar of each is unmarked. The second bars in these examples are given with the added detail necessary for a performance in which the listener hears what is happening rhythmically. In the fourth example added dynamics would be mistaken, as the strong (but missing beat) is silent. Here the notes must be played as evenly as possible in order to avoid suggestion of a false beat.

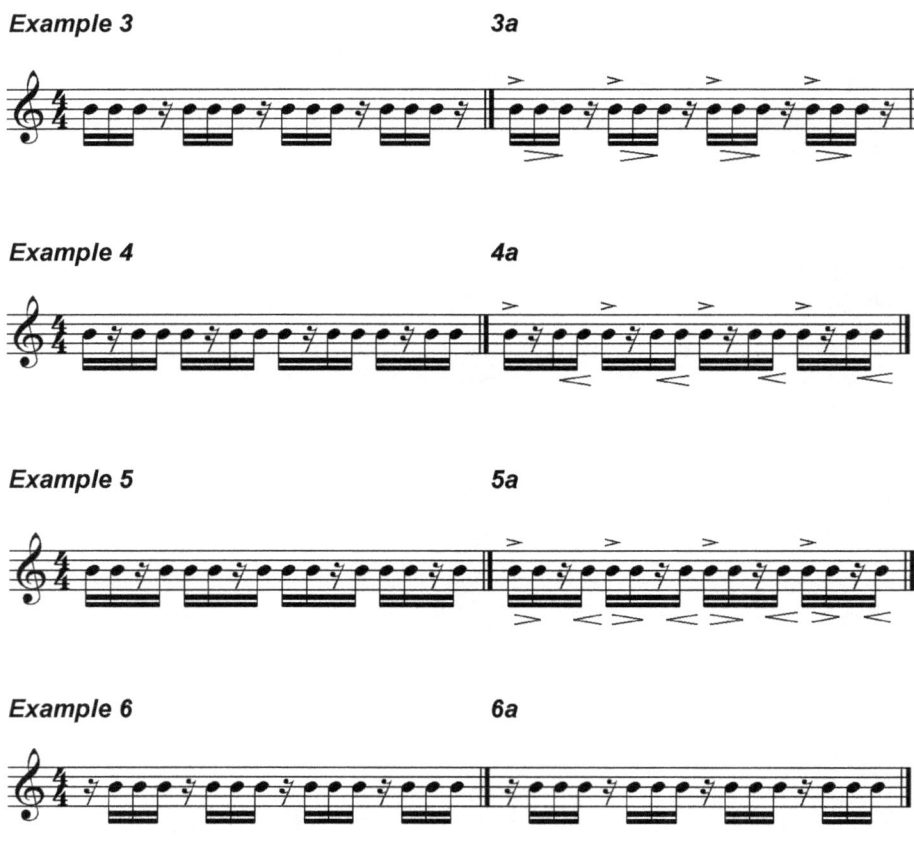

Time and rhythm: related matters

Rubato

This refers to variation of a main tempo, usually in expressive, melodic music. All parts, whether leading or following, stay together. Historically this is incorrect, when measured against the formulation made by Chopin: that ***rubato*** involves a variable melody or solo line above an accompaniment that remains in strict time. Popular singers, however, still use this form of ***rubato***: in the late twentieth century Frank Sinatra, Ella Fitzgerald, and Mel Torme used it with enormous skill, and others are still using it today.

Even when ***rubato*** is not actively in play, there are still continuous, if minute and hardly noticeable deviations from metronomic time. These variations are the life and soul of the expression. There is a direct parallel here in the way that we speak, with natural variations of pitch and volume that give full meaning to our words. This is what is missing in the words on the page of a book, and the notes on the score.

Tempo (and pulse)

Tempo denotes the speed of a passage of music, whether a complete movement or not. All tempi vary slightly as they proceed, both for musical reasons, and the demands of performing. This is linked to the idea of 'pulse' as a musical term, with its human meaning of varied regularity, its heartbeat.

Choosing a tempo is the single most important decision a performer takes about a piece of music: it controls and influences everything. With few exceptions, fast tempi should be internally steady, while slow tempi must always flow. Rhythm will then remain clear.

> *In a letter Beethoven confirmed his view, that tempo should fluctuate according to variation in the music's feelings.*

Often the inexperienced student thoughtlessly sets a tempo, only to find it unsustainable. Some let a tempo slacken to a comfortable jog, while others hurry anxiously, usually because they are not listening, but looking out for the next problem.

The maintenance of tempo

Unless there is a specific slowing down required, by a ***rallentando*** or a ***ritardando,*** or by a casual ***rubato***, always play <u>towards</u> the next major beat. This attitude of alertness to the onwards progress of the tempo, whether fast or slow, leaves the player well positioned to deal with complications of syncopation or technique. The player counting <u>from</u> the last major beat is very often late in the final parts of bars, having to scurry to catch up lost time.

Ensemble

Performers in a good ensemble have similar feelings for time and rhythm: it wouldn't be good otherwise. Orchestras consider this vital when filling a vacant chair. The potential candidate must 'feel' the relationships between notes in the same way the section does.

Further tempo matters

Accelerandi or ***rallentandi*** make their best effect when applied later rather than earlier. Do not bolt at the first sight of an '***accel***,' or brake at a '***rall***' or a '***rit***!' The same applies to ***crescendi*** and ***diminuendi***.

The beat usually means metronomic, mechanical time as heard in rock and pop music. Machines are increasingly being used for the percussion parts in popular music, as they are better at being machines than are humans! While the 'beat' in jazz is generally much more exact than 'tempo' in classical music, time in jazz is played by humans, thus maintaining its human feeling and flexibility.

Losing the plot. When players worry about 'the first note' they often lose the exact 'when' of the entry. Inevitably an inaccurate articulation follows. This then throws out time and rhythm. I repeat that if the musician imagines the sound and articulation before playing, what is wanted will, with patient repetition, come out reliably. If it is slow in coming it must be done again and again. There is no alternative to mastering this process, whether it takes five minutes or five years.

Off-the-beat entries, especially after short rests in fast tempi, should be auralised (imagined) accurately. Uncertainty often leads to an uncontrolled, explosive accent on the first note – which should be unaccented. This uncontrolled start then throws the player and the ensemble. A useful rule in these situations is as follows: start early and then relax. See ***Example 6*** above for an off-the-beat rhythm which can be awkward to perform at speed, if the player is, firstly, unclear about the placement of the notes, and secondly, the time it takes to complete the physical preparation to play whether with bow or breath. The ***Example 3*** presents no problem to the player. ***Example 6***, which is identical except for its placement in the bar, can cause instability as the player tries to hold on to the pulse.

Ambiguous rhythms By its very nature, rhythm always goes to or from a point, in a way that sometimes may not be technically convenient for the player – breath points for wind and brass players, sustaining long notes meaningfully for string players. A couple of examples, where rhythmic and melodic phrasing are often wrongly played, because of awkwardness for breathing, or thoughtless bowings, are as follows:

Example 7 – Tschaikowsky: Symphony No 4. (1st Mvmt.)

The final theme in the last movement of Sibelius' Second Symphony contains a phrase that goes to the barline. It is usually played wrongly because, for wind and brass players, the phrasing contradicts the obvious place to breathe. The breathing convenience usually wins. It is a rare conductor who notices it: Sir John Barbirolli was one.

Changes of ***tempi***, ***ritardandi***, ***rallentandi*** and ***accelerandi***, dynamics, extreme range and changes of sequence, all cause trouble for the unwary. Players can also lose track of the pulse while worrying about details and difficulties ahead; for example, even good players can lose the pulse in trills and ornaments, due to anxiety about fitting them in.

> Today I hear a lot of boring and uninteresting playing from otherwise brilliant young technicians. Rhythmic, melodic and especially articulative subtlety have diminished among the generality of younger student players. My fear is that many have been musically brainwashed, and their talents pasteurised by the commercial side of pop culture.

Pulse time versus mechanical time

Pulse Time and Mechanical Time are in deadly opposition. The first refers to conscious, active, varying human response – to traditional serious music, light music, and jazz. The second refers to the unconscious, passive response of the nervous system – to minimalist, and modern popular music. In both the serious and the vernacular music of the Western World, the **pulse is felt internally, in the mind.** It is not imposed, mechanically, from outside the music; it comes from within the music. Against the background of a tempo, the pull and push of pulse time creates energy and forward motion. Many fine classical musicians, for example, cannot dance to save their lives, which does not mean in the slightest that they are un-rhythmic in performance.

In the late twentieth century, the **exterior application of mechanical time** to music came to dominate popular music to an extraordinary degree. Layers of rhythm, which plug directly into the nervous system of the listener, are now what most popular music is about.

If you are what you eat, equally you are (musically) what you listen to

The listening diet of most young people is now dominated by pop music. In addition, the beats and back-beats of commercial muzak are constantly drip-fed, in almost all public places, as a chewing gum for the ears. This means that there is a substantial imbalance in favour of music where the components of time and rhythm are mechanical and explicit, as opposed to music where time and rhythm are human and implicit. Feeling for the expressive, flexible pulse is being driven out.

For students of classical music, this is massive over-exposure to a musical language alien to the one they are supposed to be mastering. Too much mechanical music, as opposed to human music, permanently damages the listening habits and performing responses of students of formative age. The language of European classical music is now becoming a poor second musical language for most of today's young people.

TIME PATTERNS

If these exercises are used a little but often they will have a significant effect on security, reading and performance. Accurate time and rhythm are important for three reasons:

1. The purposeful timing of notes co-ordinates all parts of the playing system, directing them to work together, with the same reactions.

2. An ability to play time and rhythm accurately and instantly, in any tempo, is the basis of professional level sight-reading. Learn how to handle times and rhythms that both interlock and compete.

3. Professional ensemble work requires the highest quality (a) of timing, i.e. the metronomically accurate placing of notes, (b) of rhythm, i.e. the shaping of groups of notes in the bar-context, and (3) of control of articulation and sound. All players in an ensemble must feel these elements in the same way for there to be coherent ensemble.

The first bars look easy, even for the beginner, but very few students will be able to play them with the accuracy which professional work requires. The development of discerning listening is not helped by just casually playing through them.

These time patterns can be played by two players, or by one player using a metronome to set the time.

- The players should play different pitches, which then can be varied into all ranges.
- Play each bar many times, listening intently for every detail.
- Once competence has improved, string several bars together.
- Constantly vary the tempi and the dynamics, as both affect time and rhythm. Also play them **accelerando** and **rallentando**. Use them on scales and arpeggios for another dimension. Exercise the imagination!
- If the result sounds acceptable, listen again, even more intently. Almost certainly there is always more to be heard.
- 99.9% of those who look at these patterns will underestimate the difficulty of playing them well, and the improvement it will bring to their technique. The same percentage will overestimate the current state of their technical capability.

Example 8

The Foreground – Melody Playing, Phrasing & Articulation

42 The Foreground – Melody Playing, Phrasing & Articulation

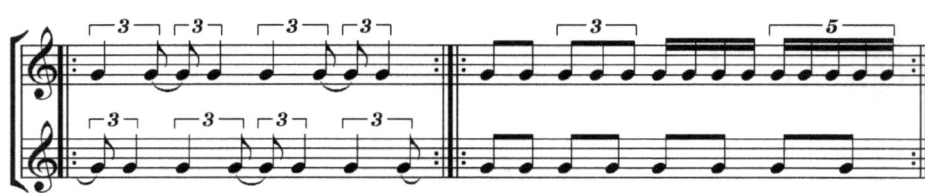

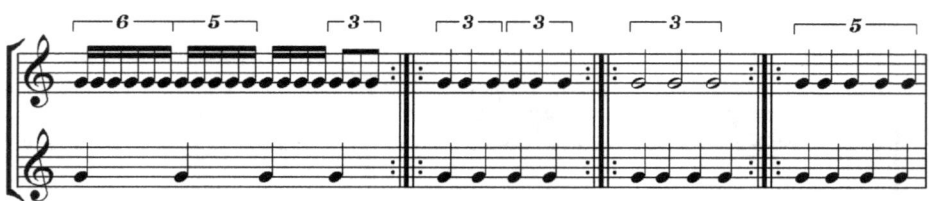

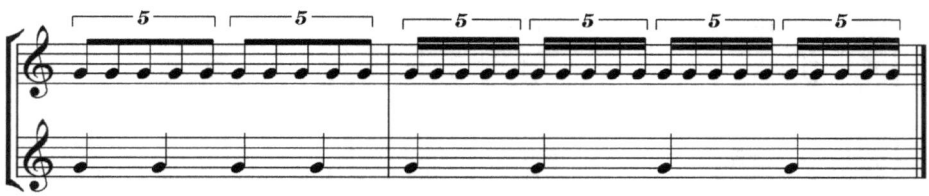

MELODY PLAYING, PHRASING & ARTICULATION

The nature of melody, phrasing, articulation etc.

A melody is a sequence of phrases that has a beginning, a continuation and an end, and has a clear musical identity. The number of phrases is variable and *legato expressivo* in slow to moderate speeds is the usual style. (A phrase is a melodic shape not extensive enough to have completeness.) A single mood dominates, even though it can vary during longer melodies. This complete-in-itself, enclosed shape, is most people's idea of a melody.

Each of the phrases that make up a melody has its own phrase point, usually at the main cadence. The phrase point is the note or notes towards which the phrase naturally aims. Each phrase may or may not have a number of minor phrasing points. Final phrase points are most often long notes that then fall away a little in volume after completion. Occasionally, after this climactic point, a small group of notes can lead away to an unemphasised conclusion, like an afterthought.

> *Artur Schnabel, the German pianist, felt strongly that there is a positive, strengthening character to an upwards-moving line, and a passive, weakening feeling to the opposite, downwards one.*

Smoothness of line is the priority in melodic playing. It gives wholeness and simplicity of effect. Yes, there are many melodies of a lively nature and *non-legato* in style, but in general avoid over-strong detailing unless there is a very good reason.

Phrasing

Phrasing shapes a melody or melodic line by varying its time and volume in amounts too small to be notated. Subtle pushing and pulling of the *tempo* and the detailing – the dynamics and the articulations – reveal our expressive response to the music. Expert phrasing can make a moderate melody seem better than it really is. It is the height of professionalism to be able to make an ordinary piece of music sound good. When playing routine melodic studies the player must treat them as if they are of musical value.

Articulation

Articulation is the detailing of notes and their connection or separation. Although the word is often used in a limited form to describe the starts of notes, articulation covers the whole subject of the presentation of notes, whether within a melodic phrase or not.

The primary forms are *legato* and *staccato*, the connected and the separated, the contrast of singing and dancing. Within those two forms are the unlimited variations of length and the application of dynamics to notes. To understand the way articulation is handled, consider the make-up of a note: it has three parts, the relationships of which are infinitely variable.

- The start of the note is important both for its timing - the when-to-play-it factor - and for its kind of articulation - the how-to-play-it factor. Timing the start of notes well – the 'when'– co-ordinates the physical actions of playing. Rhythm – the 'how' – is created by the way the notes are played, the minute relative changes in the dynamics of successive notes. In a short note the start is the critical element. Precision matters.
- The body of the note carries the sound quality of the note, and, when long enough, any written changes in dynamic. In melodic music, the body of the note is the most important part, the start and the end being less prominent. Tone quality is paramount.
- The ending of the note, like the start of the note, is important for the when-to-stop and the how-to-stop. In rhythmic music, the timing and clarity of the release of medium and long notes is almost as important as its start.

The subject of articulation is discussed further in its own chapter, next, and in the chapters on interpretation.

A melodic line

A melodic line has the characteristics of a melody, but not necessarily with a clear beginning or end. It can be as little as two notes (see Motif below) or very long indeed, with multiple phrases. Unlike an enclosed melody, its character can change dramatically as it proceeds.

A theme

A theme can be either a melody, or a melodic line long enough to develop a clear character. It is usually of primary importance in its piece of music, and provides the composer with material for development. Many instrumental lines and themes can be angular in the extreme, particularly in modern music. Try to maintain a sense of continuity even where the pitch-line is very broken.

Example 9 – Haydn: Piano Sonata No 60

A motif

A motif is usually a fragment of a melodic line or a very short theme. Its chief characteristic is its very obvious identity whenever played.

Achieving a good melodic line

- The main characteristic of good melody playing is a smooth sostenuto line. (See the section on Phrasing above.) Imagine (auralise) the sound and its feeling during the moment before playing. Once produced, carry the sound through each succeeding note rather than thinking of each as a new one. In this way your quality of sound will be heard at its best, as a single uninterrupted line.

- Use your imagination to find the character of the melody or line, in order to show it to its best advantage. **Rubato** must be within the natural boundaries of the tempo, and dynamic variations must be within the composer's markings. **Vibrato** must fit the character of the melody, and not be used indiscriminately, note by note.

> *The widespread habit of mixing vibrato and non-vibrato notes indiscriminately, prevents good phrasing, defaces the melodic line, and hides the performer's tonal personality. Good presentation of the line should be foremost in all melodic performance.*

- For instruments that breathe, choose breathing places that do not damage the composer's phrasing of the melodic line.

- For instruments that bow, choose bowings for the music's expression and not for playing convenience.

- If a breath must be taken mid-phrase, do not diminuendo into the breath. Keep it full in order to create a bridge to the note that comes after the breath. Carry the listener's attention across the gap. For those instruments that don't 'breathe' the principle is the same.

- When a melody or line is shared, knowingly hand it over to the incoming player. When taking over a melodic line, it is equally good musical manners to maintain the expression in the same style as the previous player.

- Take care of shorter notes. In slower melodies, keep them broad in length and sound: they carry the melodic flow as much as the more obvious longer notes. In quicker music they must always be clear, and never gabbled.

- When working to find the character of a melody, play it through in different transpositions, as if looking at an object from different angles in order to really know it. Invent new and interesting phrasings and always try fresh ideas. Although words and sentences do not offer an exact parallel with a musical phrase, a simple sentence shows how phrasing can change meaning. Take a simple sentence – '<u>The</u> cat sat on the mat' – then move the emphasis along, word by word, finally adding a question mark. Watch the meaning constantly change. While music obviously does not hold meaning as words do, changing the phrase points reshapes the musical meaning.

- Good rhythm is vital to any melody, even when the mood is quiet and gentle. The progression of notes **towards** strong beats and minor phrase points are often neglected, because insecure performers tend to count **from** the previous strong beat or barline. This latter habit leads to dragging. Except when relaxing from the main phrase point, always try to **play towards** the phrase point: the climax point of most phrases occurs at or near their end.

- Masters of long, slow melodies and melodic lines, such as Bach or Rachmaninov, play with rhythm and mood as a means to sustain interest. The chapter on articulation deals with the details that add further shaping within phrases.

- Turns of mood, as revealed by harmony, are equally worthy of attention, in the search for better performance. Study of the great masters' music will repay you many times over as you search for better melodic understanding.

> *The beautiful upbeat* - When a melody has an upbeat, it is rare, today, to hear it played well. Rather than being presented as a welcoming invitation to listen to a melody, it is often treated charmlessly, almost always without vibrato, as if the player has his attention on the notes that are ahead, and not on the note being played.

- Full beauty of tone is often masked by playing into the music stand, especially when playing softly. Make sure the listener receives all the qualities of the sound that you have to offer.

- Practise melodic passages much slower than written. In this way you have time to develop awareness of living tone quality separate to the demands of the normal context.

A simple exercise

The following phrase contains two minor, and two major emphasis points. Playing the phrase on one pitch, as in the first version, guides the player's attention to the shaping of the notes towards these points. The second version uses an adjacent note to bring in slurring. The third gives the actual phrase. This exercise is akin to miming – a dumb melody!

Example 10

ARTICULATION
(or The Presentation of Detail)

Types

As discussed in the chapter on Time & Rhythm, the word articulation has a number of meanings. Musicians tend to use the word without making clear which meaning is being used at any one time. This is why I refer to it as the presentation of detail, which is what it is. Articulation can be:

- The start, or end of a note, whether accented, unaccented or otherwise characterised,
- The connection or disconnection of notes, the legato and staccato of notes, with variations, or
- The internal shaping of a note, however broadened, slimmed down, or otherwise managed.

Starts, Stops and Shapes

On most instruments where the pitch of each note has to be made, e.g. the violin – as opposed to those where the note is largely made already, e.g. the piano – the first note spells some danger. In truth, many musicians only play wholeheartedly once the launch process has been achieved. (See the insertion note on 'the beautiful upbeat' in the previous chapter.) This fear-ridden process contributes greatly to the anxiety that plagues many players.

Accept the danger. In fact, welcome it, as part of the risk of being a musician. Safe danger? – Not possible! The danger of performance can draw responses from your inner, unknown, unrealised talent.

Shaping individual notes is part of phrasing, as discussed in the chapter on Melody. To see examples of a very wide range of articulations, glance at any score by Mahler, for example. It will offer the most comprehensive illustration of the possibilities available.

Achieving different articulations

Just as we speak lovingly, angrily or calmly as the emotion of the moment demands, your vocal chords shape the consonants and vowels to express feelings. Compare the ways you would say 'Damn' in annoyance, or 'Darling' to a loved one.

Similarly, your mind will prepare your body to take the actions necessary to play the way you want. Follow your musical idea, without concern for mistakes. Worrying about every error, and gritting your teeth in the hope of producing perfection, will simply block progress. (You'll only become good at worrying and gritting your teeth!)

Articulation, tempo and technique

The length of articulation used in a particular passage must be appropriate for its tempo. This particularly applies to crotchets (quarter-notes) and their subdivisions. A simple rule suffices:

- If the passage drags, the note-lengths are too long.
- If the passage rushes, the note-lengths are too short.

Both these situations create technical problems. Dragging often produces faulty tone control and distension of the melodic line. Rushing tends to produce the same effect as driving a car too fast around a slippery corner! Anxious players are often unaware of their own rushing or dragging.

DYNAMICS

General issues

- Assess your own habits, strengths and weaknesses. Dynamics are often treated as the poor relations compared to pitches and rhythms, and are generally dealt with very casually or even carelessly. Musicians generally pay as much attention to dynamics as the public pays to speed limits!
- Knowing the requirements of different periods of music, composers, and their styles, places a further responsibility on the performer.

Specific issues

- Setting levels for each work performed.
- Control over variations of dynamics and accompanying detail.

Developing soft dynamics

Soft dynamics mercilessly expose gaps in playing technique on any instrument. Force cannot be used to solve awkward problems in *piano,* as it sometimes can in louder dynamics. Try the following:

- Play a long note or short phrase at *mezzoforte*, concentrating on the sense of physical comfort and musical effect. Repeat a little softer, taking care that the effort you are putting in remains the same as at *mezzoforte.* This is vital. Repeat, slightly softer, maintaining the same level of comfortable physical action. Continue till *pianissimo* is reached. At all times keep the sound full: thin sound is not a substitute for soft sound, is unreliable under pressure, and is unpleasant to the ear.

> *The halls and platforms in which we perform affect our use of dynamics. Not only do their shapes and sizes change our intended playing, but the harsh surfaces of modern building materials, used by architects without any musical culture, provide a very hostile environment for the musician in most newer halls. When I arrive to perform in an unknown hall, I experience immediate relief if it is an 'older' one!*

- If at any point the simplest, smoothest effort to play becomes hindered, go back to the last level where you felt comfortable. Repeat the process, very gradually, in order to gain control of your input.

- Then introduce ***diminuendi***, and ***crescendi,*** going right down into the scarcely audible zone. Then spread out into all pitch ranges as your comfort and command grows.

The vital point is to maintain the same kind of physical effort in a soft dynamic as in a medium or loud dynamic. Anxious squeezing of the muscular system is the commonest reason for poor ***piani*** and ***pianissimi***. Anxiety creates it: therefore it sounds anxious.

Developing loud dynamics

Cultivate a smooth, unforced delivery. Produce your best quality sound at all times and in all dynamics. Work from ***mezzoforte*** to ***fortissimo***, but in this process upwards, use ***diminuendi*** and ***crescendi*** from the start. Be sure to produce your best sound quality: if a good sound starts to 'scream' under the pressure to become louder, retreat and do more work just below the threshold where it starts to distort.

Developing dynamic control

Accurate control can only be achieved by training your ear to discern every conceivable shade in the dynamic spectrum.

Approaching individual works

Historically the detail offered by composers in their scores has become progressively more complex over time. Scores from earlier periods of music show very few markings. Not until the latter half of the eighteenth century do we see composers' wishes expressed in any detail. Examine each score to assess the composer's personal use of markings: they are always revealing.

Debussy set new levels of precision in the use of dynamics. But rather than demanding exact responses, he prompts us to re-create the illusion that he has conceived. His use of dynamic signs suggests touch and mood as well as volume, but even he rarely wrote down piano pedallings, preferring to trust the musician's imagination.

Many composers of the latter part of the twentieth century have filled their scores with unrealistically complicated demands regarding dynamics, both from the point of view of the player, the listener and the random nature of the acoustic in which a piece is performed.

> *The young musician almost never understands how difficult it is to play really correctly. That means not only finger-technically but also expression-technically, exactly according to the wishes of the composer.*
>
> Walter Gieseking

Establishing levels

Play the main dynamics of the work on one note in order to set their levels, otherwise you will find yourself being haphazard. Where a particular passage has detailed, demanding or confusing marks, the same strategy works well: play passages on one note until fluency is achieved. If necessary, firstly play without time or rhythm with every note the same length. Then play in time, finally adding the pitches. Some composers can be very unrealistic in their markings, so decide what is practical as well as desirable. In the case of a complicated score, read through it without the instrument until your eye is comfortable with it.

Remember also that the composer's motive may vary. The extreme detail of Mahler's and Elgar's scores suggests precision, whereas the **ffff** and **pppp** that is found in Verdi and Tschaikovsky suggest desperate attempts to force contemporary players to play both softer and louder. Similarly with note lengths, the unrealistic demi-semi-quavers (32nds) found in Bruckner's Symphonies suggests the composer begging the players 'Don't be so lazy! Please play shorter and later!'

Why are dynamics so important?

Sensitivity to dynamics is not only an element in realising composers' wishes. At the level of the unwritten content of music – detail too fine to be notated, that composers expect to be understood – the proper inflexions (articulations) are essential. Every period of music has its own language, every composer his own sound world.

Dynamics and balance

Are you the leading voice? Or are you a secondary counterpoint to the solo? Are you an important accompanying element, with critical harmonic touches that need to be briefly brought out at key moments? Or is your part a minor filling in the sandwich?

Music is largely a social activity: balance in ensemble is one of the key factors when musicians work together. Awareness of your constantly varying team role in an ensemble work is essential to becoming a good performer.

Pianists, guitarists and other lone soloists must solve all these matters internally. Single line instrumentalists co-operate with others to fulfil a composer's wishes.

INTONATION

What's the Problem?

Natural tuning vs. Equal Temperament tuning within the octave.

What is 'natural tuning'?

Natural tuning, or how the ear likes to hear intervals within keys, was the basis of numerous tuning systems until the seventeenth century. The ear's preference for 'unequal' intervals – such as pure fifths (sharp) and pure thirds (flat) – persists to this day, in spite of hundreds of years experience of equal temperament.

In the context of a particular key, sensitive players adjust the 'same' note in varying chordal situations. A *G#* is not an *Ab,* except on a fixed pitch instrument! Watch a fine trombonist make minute adjustments to slide positions for the 'same' note in different chords. In making these enharmonic changes the player responds to the needs of natural tuning. Conversely, string players may take easier fingerings from the 'wrong' key, when those from the 'right' key are more difficult, i.e. an *Ab* will be used when it should be a *G#*. In the case of valved brass instrumentalists, false (alternative) fingerings in appropriate situations are commonplace, to meet the shifting demands of ensemble tuning.

> *My description of a conflict among musicians, thinkers and artists that raged back and forth for a couple of hundred years, is a very simplified one indeed. For example, as keyboard design evolved in the 17th century, theorists squashed in up to 27 keys per octave to fit in natural (or just) tunings.*
>
> Mersenne: Harmonie Universelle

'Equal temperament'?

Equal temperament, in which the octave is divided into twelve equal semitones, emerged as the victor over many other different systems just prior to the lifetime of J.S. Bach. Musicians had become aware of a possible palette of twelve interlocking key centres and of course wanted to use it. Bach's two sets of Preludes and Fugues in all the major and minor keys, the 'Forty-Eight', stand as the earliest and greatest monument to the concept of equal temperament.

Prior to the development of equal semitone tuning, key centres existed separately from each other with limited movement to related keys. Natural tuning makes it excruciating to go beyond three or four keys distant from the home key. Free modulation – the capacity to side-track into any key, near or far, gradually or instantly – was therefore not practical as we now know it. The possibilities opened up by modulation must have been the musical equivalent of the change from the flat-earth to the round-earth theory in astronomy, or the development of perspective in painting.

Why the conflicts?

The tuning of all instruments, except those of fixed pitch, is a compromise, whether for the violinist who tunes in pure (sharp fifths), or for the brassist who chooses a basic tube length that will fit most, but not all notes. Both have to juggle, not only with the technical demands of the instrument, but two factors that are ever-present and demand a flexible response:

- the horizontal progression of the notes, and at the same time.
- the vertical harmony.

Melodic issues ~ or how notes 'tend' in the horizontal

A melodic line, together with its harmony, is always 'going to' or 'coming from', 'aiming at', or 'resolving from' a phrase point or climax. For example, the leading note, the seventh of a scale tends – needs – to resolve upwards to the tonic. The fourth tends downwards to the third. And so on. The prevailing tonality controls these senses of direction. If a modulation takes the music to a new key, even temporarily, the intonation relates to that new key.

When an instrument plays alone it is more difficult to judge a note's intonation, as there is no obvious harmonic background available for comparisons to be made. However, any horizontal progression of notes builds up an harmonic context. The ear remembers the trail of notes left by the instrument, synthesises them into a context, and then matches each new one to that context. Develop sensitivity to these horizontal relationships: don't just wait until alerted by an obviously bad fault. General improvement always follows awareness, as night follows day.

Harmonic issues ~ or how intervals stack up vertically

Every interval has a tuning width that the ear likes. This remnant of natural tuning shows itself most clearly in the bright (sharp) fifth heard most commonly during the tuning of a violin. Most fifths on the piano are flat.

The *unison* and the *octave* are precise intervals: the ear demands that they ring exactly. When perfect they are unmatched for beauty and sonority. Thereafter, to my ear, intervals go in matching pairs within the octave, usually, but not always, one sharper and one flatter.

- The *perfect fifth* is unmistakable when true. In nature, it is sharper than equal temperament (piano tuning) allows. The choice of the orchestral tuning *A,* allows the violins to take a level conveniently central to their string configuration, and then tune down to the *D* and *G*, then up to the *E*. This is proven when a cycle (progression) of perfectly tuned fifths is played upwards. Were violins to tune up in naturally bright fifths from the low *G*, the resulting fourth string *E* would be extremely sharp – and often is! A cycle of natural fifths tuned upwards from the lowest piano **A** would end with an impossibly sharp **A** twelve intervals higher. Its opposite, the **perfect fourth**, is a narrow interval. As the fourth in the scale it tends downwards towards the third, whether major or minor. An upwards cycle of well-tuned fourths would be very flat. All cycles of twelve notes end sharp or flat.

♦ The matching thirds and sixths are the most negotiable of the pairings. In natural tuning the major third is almost always happiest when very slightly flat. If a series of three natural major thirds were tuned, say, C to E, E to G#, Ab to C, the resultant octave C to C would be flat. Compare this with the cycle of perfect fifths mentioned above. (In the context of an augmented triad, the thirds stretch upwards a little in order to express the uptending of the interval's direction.) To my ear the minor sixth can vary a lot according to its place in whichever key. Similarly the minor third and its pair the major sixth are variable according to context, although officially the minor third should be on the sharp side.

♦ The major second is a full strong up-tending interval, whereas its match, the minor seventh, is a down-tending interval, like the perfect fourth.

♦ The minor second is a narrow down-tending interval, partnering the bright up-tending major seventh.

♦ The augmented fourth/diminished fifth divides the octave exactly in half, and is the only perfect pair within it.

Chords of three notes are the commonest, but chords of four or more notes are very frequently used. The middle and lower parts of these complex chords are where tuning problems lurk. The controlling note of any chord is the lowest: all others relate to it. If the highest voice in any group sounds flat, check the lowest pitch in the chord first. In order to make some upper tunings fit, it may be necessary to lower the pitch of the bass note much more than can initially be believed.

General matters

How is the same note in different keys managed?

As mentioned earlier, a note will have a different slant according to the key in which it lives. A **G#** in the key of **A major** (the seventh) will need to sound sharper than an **Ab** (the fourth) in the key of **Eb major**. These unequal relationships within a key must be understood by the ear before playing of the highest quality can be achieved. In addition to the unnatural evenness of twelve equal tones, most evident in piano tuning, many wind and brass instruments' harmonic series, in which some notes are flatter and some sharper, criss-cross randomly with the tuning configurations required by the key of the music. The natural lie of brass instrument pitch was lost as soon as instruments became valved and therefore chromatic. The result is that often the

> *Unless notated or unavoidable, string players will avoid the raw quality of open strings. The open sound is quite different in quality to fingered notes.*

natural tuning of the note on the brass instrument (the harmonic series) is wrong for the pitch of the note required by the musical context (the key).

How does tone affect tuning?

Wind, and particularly, valved brass instruments, must be aware of changes of tone colour when choosing a fingering for tuning purposes. A random bright or dull sound out of context can spoil a phrase.

How to tune with the piano

The piano is the most difficult partner for instruments where players make the pitch. Not only does the artificial equality of pitch fight any chosen tonality, but pianos are generally tuned to A = 440, just below the pitch at which orchestral instruments normally play. When preparing a recital with a piano, bring the pitch of your instrument – and your ear – down several weeks before a concert. Attempt it at the last moment and you will be too late. Your ear, your memory of pitch, will keep the pitch level up. In addition, take care to match important exposed notes with the piano, i.e. notes that are longer, on the stronger beats and at extremes of pitch. A piano is totally unforgiving in its tuning. Matching the tuning of pianos in the accompaniment of concerti can often be a great difficulty, particularly for woodwind soloists in the orchestra. The poor Principal Oboe giving the orchestral **'A'** has to take all the flak when trying to square this particular circle.

How rhythm, note lengths and intonation interact

Quality of intonation is most noticeable on longer notes and on the main beats of the bar. For example, in a 4/4 bar, the notes occurring on the first and third beats have the clearest audibility. In groupings of semiquavers (sixteenths), the first of each group is the most audible, because the most dominant rhythmically.

The importance of good intonation

Be aware of intonation all the time, and understand the response of our listening faculties. The finer our tuning, the cleaner and more enjoyable will be the impression we give. Good intonation, timing and rhythm are all parts of essential musical hygiene.

Tuning groups of instruments

My system of tuning a group of players of the same instrument is as follows:

- One by one, play a named note, being sure to have a silence between each player. The space allows a comparison to be heard. Playing together does not. Initially, do not alter basic tuning.
- Repeat the process, with a succession of four or five other notes.
- By this point, it will be clear which players are in tune, flatter, or sharper. Prompt each one to identify the problems for themselves, thus developing their own sense of intonation and their personal responsibility for it.

- Continue, but not for long! It is easy to become confused by tuning matters. Best to achieve a small improvement, and then return to the subject at frequent intervals.

- With a group of players on diverse instruments, adopt the same process, but first tune the principal players of each section on a mixture of unisons and octaves. These players can then test their own groups separately.

> ***Electronic Tuning Devices*** *- These are not for the serious musician! For the reasons given above, they are inaccurate for all but the crudest purposes. They remove from the musician the responsibility for listening, judging and refining his sense of pitch. These machines are a good example of technology's main purpose, which is to de-skill the human race, and reduce it to mindless slavery and dependancy!*

INTERPRETATION: 1

Interpretation defined

Interpretation is the act of imagination needed to turn a composer's score into a performance. We read the notes, and decide what they mean. We judge the composer's intentions, what is non-negotiable in the score, and what are the freer elements that allow some leeway and spontaneity. After absorbing the work, and synthesising our ideas, we try to bring about an effective performance.

It is all too easy to take the elements of music for granted. For example, harmony and rhythm can be thought boring if they lack fashionable spice and piquancy. Understanding and appreciation of harmony – how it is set in its key, and then on a wider scale, how the keys and their colours are juxtaposed via a web of modulations – can give invaluable clues as to the composer's intentions.

Only when we fully know the composer's intentions, can we start to interpret properly. No work of value is just a series of chance events that may or may not be momentarily pleasing. Every note or instruction a composer writes reveals an intention. Look at all the elements – pitch, harmony, rhythm, dynamics and articulation. Look at the scoring textures and sonorities used. Every detail speaks volumes if only we take the trouble to look.

> **Composers & Metronomes!** – The first word that springs to mind is *'unreliable'*! Since they were invented in Beethoven's time, they have been more trouble than they are worth. Firstly, composers always 'think' their music at a different speed to which they perform it. (When Stravinsky was asked why he conducted his music much faster that his metronome marks, he suddenly revealed that they were minimum markings - never having mentioned it before! A great composer, he was a very moderate conductor as I know from personal experience.) The more exact some composers' written instructions the less exact their performance, it seems. Also, their ideas about their music can change greatly over the years. What really matters are the relationships <u>between</u> **tempi** within a work or a movement.

The tools to use

Every piece, good or bad, long or short, has a musical story through it, a musical line. Follow the line through every work as it would have been conceived by the composer. 'But how do you know?' I hear the question asked. 'Experience and judgement!' is the answer. The experience of reading and listening to countless scores and performances, and judging the success and failure of each through honest comparison. I use the word 'honest' deliberately: too often we can find excuses for our own failings, but none for others'.

Take in the texture of the scoring, the melodic and rhythmic shapes used. Be aware of the harmony as it tightens then relaxes, and particularly plot how the composer uses modulation to change the mood gradually or suddenly, and control the listeners' emotions. In larger works I think of the story as an odyssey, a coming home after a long journey. Many sights, detours and other attractions occur along the way, but they are all part of the journey.

For mood, we can use the associations of images and adjectives. For *legato* Mozart liked the image of pouring oil. Another person might like to think of the feel of silk under the fingers or the movement of fish through water. For you, the most powerful image for any musical situation – *legato, scherzando* and so on – is the one you find inside your own mind. For example, what is your image of smoothness? Can you transfer it to your playing? Composers do use adjectives to describe mood, but they are so general it is easy to overlook them.

Other people's ideas: compare and contrast

When you have firm ideas about a piece, then – and only then – listen to a number of recordings by different performers: your appreciation of the options will improve. Note the relative success of the performances, and how each performer shapes the piece and handles its details. Note key points such as tempi, sound, note lengths, accentuations, slurrings, ornamentation and cadenzas.

Then review your own ideas with an open mind, not merely to congratulate yourself. Attempt to imitate performance details, such as articulations and phrasings, that are different to your own. You will find that these efforts will reveal a great deal about your own playing, and enhance your own responses. But, in the end, your interpretation must be honestly your own. How else will you develop yourself, and increase your own resources, except by your own trial and error? You cannot thumb a lift to short-cut to experience. Every step has to be walked.

> *Never be carried away by (your) temperament, because it dissipates strength of mind.*
>
> Busoni

The treatment of detail

For the treatment of detail, remember what you are like as a person, and how your own tastes work. Do you like variety in your life? Then make sure your performance shows variety. Your audience is also looking for stimulus. Contrast and unity, more and less – whether speed or volume – tension and relaxation, these pairings of words describe the stimuli we all need in order to maintain our interest in things. Just running through the notes is not enough.

With these ideas in mind, we can vary phrases, motives and articulations so that the music is constantly heard from a different angle.

Individuality! Who needs it?

Do not concern yourself with individuality, or confuse your ego with intelligence. A reverse law is in operation here: the more anonymous you try to be in dealing with interpretation, the more your true individuality will emerge. A lot of musicians speak about playing 'as I feel it', or 'as the moment takes me', as if referring to the wonderful internal artist that the listener cannot appreciate but only worship with awe from afar. Nuts! No interpretation of value can take place without knowledge and consideration. Only certain limited elements of music can be dealt with spontaneously. Better to use experience and understanding than trust to some ill-defined, sloppy piece of chance. There is no intrinsic value in being oneself: it is what one knows that is of value.

> *Play to reveal the music, not to show off.*
> *(as Busoni might also have said)*

Work with the score frequently but without the instrument. Doing that allows your mind freedom to explore options and choices that may not be obvious in the hurly-burly of playing.

Interpretation: 2

In the next chapter of the book, I offer a more detailed approach to Interpretation.

INTERPRETATION: 2

"If there is anything you don't understand in a piece of music ... sing it!"
Donald Francis Tovey

"The only sound foundation ... is ... knowledge gained as the result of personal effort and personal experience."
Heinrich Neuhaus

Building a framework for interpreting music

The suggestions that follow offer a more detailed process for creating an interpretation. After working a few pieces like this your mind and ear will start to run through it easily. Once it becomes automatic then your own ideas will develop.

Three thoughts to keep in mind:

- Melody derives from the voice. It depends on the succession of intervals.

- Rhythm derives from the body's pulse. Its life depends on the spaces between the notes, the lengths of the notes and how we use dynamics and articulations to alter the notes and their relationships.

- Articulation – the presentation of appropriate detail – is essential if any performance is going to be successful. The element of pitch is almost always set and non-negotiable. The element of time normally has degrees of flexibility of presentation. Articulation is arguably the most personal element of all: the detailing of music can be amazingly varied, while at the same time according exactly to the composer's written wishes.

The stages

♦ **Familiarisation**
This is the obvious getting-to-know-you stage. If opening up a new piece of music doesn't excite you, take up some other work! This is the easiest phase, taking in first impressions, getting a feel of the piece.

♦ **Shaping the picture – 'the artistic image'**
First of all settle on the character of the piece. A clear image of the work, however slight, will give will give you a basis. This is the first and most important matter. Every work of value has its own unique tonal landscape, in which each of the elements of music is used in an identifiable way.

Then consider **tempo** – the single most important choice for a work. This is not only a musical judgement but also a technical one. It is necessary to look at the quickest (or most difficult notes) of the piece, in order to decide a practical speed. A tempo can be slackened or tightened according to passing moods, but the underlying pulse must remain identifiably the same, unless changed by the composer. Going beyond the natural boundaries of a tempo is a serious error of judgement. In repertoire without metronome marks and only general tempo marks, examine the passages with the quickest notes. Make your final assessment only when you have considered how you want to treat them, musically and technically.

> *The expressive possibilities of articulation are unlimited. In classical music performance today, however, they are being used less and less: the standard virtuoso seems to have a handful of stock responses geared to projection and surface glamour, perhaps engendered by the steely sound perspectives of the recording industry. Many of today's 'artists' talk a great game, in the manner of sports stars, but there is a lack of variety in articulation, that excludes the delicate and the intimate. This, perhaps, is why so much contemporary performance is bland, in spite of note-playing capability being at a high level in many instruments.*

Speed of harmonic change in a piece also suggests tempo, as do subdivisions of the pulse-unit. For example, if the tempo is in crotchet (quarter-note) units, then its subdivisions will speak volumes about the composers wishes.

> *Mozart wrote that it is much easier to play a thing quickly than to play it slowly. I suppose he meant that the mistakes go past that much faster!*

Why do many players play too fast? Because they can! Because they are too familiar with the piece as a technical/manual problem, or are too accomplished manually to want to give first consideration to the expression of the music. (Everyone has done this at some time.) In one sense these players over-solve the manual problems at the expense of a piece's character. The danger is that a performance becomes little more than a speed-reading summary of a work conceived, musically speaking, long ago and far away. Many modern baroque performances sound like this.

Whether we consider melodies, melodic lines, themes or motives, detailed examination of them will yield insight into the composer's intentions. Sing them. If it is contrapuntal, sing all the lines. (See Vocalisation) The shapes and gestures of the lines will give up their phrasing secrets, their character, more readily to your voice than to any other instrument. For example, leaps of a fifth or more are not difficult

> *Modern official educational practice in schools says that this form of musical knowledge is largely unnecessary and that 'response to the experience of music' is what matters. This 'thinking' is wrong, if only because it is causing a decline in the general level of musical expertise. Young people are thus being denied the knowledge that will help them to realise their talents.*

on a piano or violin, but for the voice it is a significant gesture. There is no doubt that the composer will feel it that way. Ralph Kirkpatrick, the harpsichordist, asked his students to step out melodies on the floor in units equal to the intervals. He commented that afterwards they always sat down at the keyboard with an improved understanding of melodic movement.

- ◆ **Technical matters**

Next, decide on technical matters such as fingerings, bowings, tonguings. Also, at this point, articulation – the detailing – will come to the front of the picture.

The role of articulation is under-exploited today, and is understood only in a limited form. It refers not only to the starts of notes, but also their lengths, styles and shapes, and manner of stopping. It means the joining or the separation of notes and the innumerable variations possible between the two.

What controls these choices of length and shape? Awareness of the composer's intention via the tensions and relaxations of harmony and counterpoint. Acquiring this awareness is essential if the musician is to play competently.

Historically, articulation marks vary a good deal in their meaning. The *staccato* point in Mozart, for example, signifies only a slight marking of the note. The full dash mark, as shown in authentic Mozart editions, is the sign for a modern *staccato* to be played. Similarly, in nineteenth century repertoire, the use of the *tenuto* mark clearly denotes a full-length legato note, with a degree of stress that places it at the top end of its dynamic level. The modern version – as in Stravinsky – denotes what I call a flat accent. It is clearly accented, and squared-off slightly short in order to add rhythmic vitality. In another instance, ends of notes can be stopped rhythmically in such a way as to hand the pulse on to the next note, a slightly different effect to the modern *tenuto* mark.

Alternatively notes can be ended without clarity, or be smoothed away to nothing. Further to this, the detailing of a few notes within a legato phrase can be achieved with a *mezzo-staccato,* or with a *portato* (dragged) style.

- ◆ **Analysis**

Study the form of the piece and the presentation of themes, motives, developments, transitions and codas. How standard is the form, or is it a free shape? Decide what is important and also less important. Together with that comes the phrasing of melodies and counterpoints, the placing of climaxes as part of the consideration of dynamics.

In coping with the rhythmic difficulties of a piece, otherwise competent student players often accentuate the barline with physical movements due to rhythmic insecurity. Foot tapping and waving the instrument are common forms of this kind of self-conducting. These practices introduce very audible accents in the musical result – thus killing the phrase-shape – and almost always causing quite unnecessary playing problems.

From the beginning of the first reading of a piece, the general rhythmic character of the work will have been evident. Now search out the composer's detailed use of rhythms: this will illuminate the inner character the composer is seeking for the piece. Make sure that the patterns are audible and coherent.

Rhythm has its own counterpoints: not only in the setting of pattern against pattern, but in the placement of the same pattern in different metrical contexts. Different treatments and shapings are needed. A simple example:

Example 11: Brahms Symphony No. 3 (3rd Mvt.)

Even a slow melody has a rhythmic basis, with different layers of time values acting on each other, giving the music its particular flow. The smaller values, especially those that occur within the main beats and the upbeats, yield valuable clues.

Harmonic structure can be looked at in two ways. The big picture – charting the modulation of keys from start to finish – shows the course the piece is taking. Intensifying, relaxing, resolving – these are the kinds of sensation generated by the harmony, as the piece travels through longer stretches of time. The succession of harmonies will signpost climaxes very clearly. It is also interesting that the rise and fall of excitement of harmonic change almost always goes hand-in-hand with metrical change.

Within this big picture, individual harmonic moments reveal where the composer needs the music to be pointed up. Crucially, it is the preparation of these significant moments, that determines their success or failure. It is not so much how we handle the actual points of tension or relaxation themselves, it is the build-up. It is very instructive to play through or imagine (auralise) the chord progression of a complete piece, so that the harmony's journey is clear, both as a whole and in detail. (Both the **C major Prelude** of Book One of **Bach's '48'**, and the 4th movement, the **Via Appia**, of **Respighi's 'Pines of Rome'** give excellent examples of perfectly shaped, but very different harmonic journeys.)

Give attention also to bridge passages and transitions. They often contain some of the composer's most significant material with regard to the shaping of the piece.

When all of this has been done, in your mind return to the big picture, see the overall drama. Characterise the piece, especially with regard to an immediate personality at the start. First impressions are critical in music performance as well as life.

Serious practice

This arrives when all factors have been understood and synthesised into a unified whole. This part of the process is as short or long as the problems allow or demand. The world of practice techniques is quite separate from that of interpretation. Put your practice to the service of your musical ideas.

♦ **Absorption**

The process of absorbing your unified idea cannot be rushed, and is almost passive in nature. Regularly give the work a rest, in order to allow your subconscious to become friends with it! Trust your inner self to sort out unresolved matters ... i.e. be patient. Any piece will benefit for being left alone from time to time whether for a few days or perhaps for several weeks. Do not interfere with the process.

♦ **The maturing process**

You may have learned the piece to the point where it can be presented to everyone's satisfaction. But nothing can rush the final part of the process: the maturing of your work, via time (getting older) and contemplation (quietly thinking afresh). Of course we can wait forever for the perfect moment – there isn't one – because tomorrow, perhaps, you and I will be wiser than today. But there comes a recognisable moment, when we know that we have made a piece our own, after which, we can perform it responsibly and not as cheap speculation.

> *Success is dangerous. One begins to copy oneself, and to copy oneself is more dangerous than to copy others. It leads to sterility.*
>
> Picasso

This description of the process of interpretation is, of course, artificial: there is so much overlap between the stages of consideration of a piece of music, and so much improvisation in each individual's response to its appeal.

Living with success

If your performances are bringing you success, be sure to continue the process of frequent revision: do not be content with being fixed and predictable. No piece of music should be frozen into one interpretation.

Do not typecast yourself with a standardised response to all music. The masterpieces of music have more in them than any one person can find at any one moment. It is in the nature of music that there cannot be a definitive version of any work.

Your ideas will continue to develop and change with the passing of time. If you are a living, learning musician, both you and your responses will mature. The only constant factor in life is change, and purifying your changing vision is the only way to keep your work alive. Beware the clichés that encourage you to play 'off-the-cuff' or 'as-you-feel-it'. Much better to value the distillation of experience as your way forward.

Part Two

PRACTICE

1 : ASSEMBLING THE TOOLBOX

"Behind every kick of the ball there has to be a thought."
Dennis Bergkamp, Arsenal and Holland footballer

The five compartments of the toolbox

1. Managing yourself and your practice (Chapter 2)

What is Practice? Practice is the activity of weaving the physical and mental skills of playing into one strand, ready for performance. The nature of practice is quite different to performance and is just as demanding.

The practice room is the player's workshop. To practise effectively is arguably the hardest task faced by a musician. It is very complex: it demands intelligence, self-control and knowledge in equal measures.

2. Practice: using the musical elements (Chapters 3 – 6)

The techniques in these chapters are based on using the musical elements to expose and solve problems. They work by understanding and manipulating the elements of music – pitch, time and detail – and how they interact in any particular passage of music.

3. Practice: using alteration, distortion & simplification (Chapters 7 – 14)

We can gain control of situations that seem beyond us by altering and distorting them and by learning how to approach problems indirectly. These techniques allow us to see a problem from new angles, to reveal solutions not obvious on the surface.

4. Mental skills (Chapters 15 – 17)

Imagining sounds (Auralisation), using the voice (Vocalisation) and visualising situations (Visualisation), are not just techniques to help in solving immediate problems, or useful ways of spending time when tired of the instrument. With these techniques you can refresh and improve the whole way in which you make music. If you are brave enough you can dream up any ideas you want. Boldness creates technique.

5. Looking after yourself (Chapters 18 – 21)

When young we often think we can afford to ignore our body. It recovers fast because we are (so we are told) in the prime of life. But is that really true? Or is it a resource we abuse at our future peril?

Practice techniques: the key

First and foremost I create situations in which the player discovers. Discovers what? Discovers what he is actually playing. This then prompts him to find what he really wants to do. Prompts how? By listening intently and making comparisons and judgements, by using disciplines inherent in the music and by the inter-operation of musical elements and technical elements.

Unless a teacher wishes to impose his musical solution on a student, there is little need to use precise verbal descriptions to produce improvement. I always try to find the student musician's own answers: in fact I almost always demand that the student uses his own musical talent, or how else will it develop? What's the point of someone else's second-hand interpretation? Encouraging, questioning and channelling the student's efforts to repeat-and-listen, repeat-and-listen, are my way forward. The student can learn to do this for himself, and is thus on the way to self-sufficiency and self-reliance.

> *Every musician has to discover the basics of music performance afresh for himself. It is not possible to leapfrog hard work and experience.*

The value that I have tried to capture in this book is that listening solves most things, but if it doesn't solve a particular long-term matter it will at least identify the problem and point the way forward. Understand the problem and the answer will appear.

2: MANAGING YOUR PRACTICE

"Think ten times and play once." Franz Liszt

The expertise of practising

Practising works through expertise and know-how. The methods in this book reveal how this can be achieved, and offer the means by which your image of a piece of music can be transferred to your instrument.

Many players prefer to learn by 'just playing', which may work for the few, but for the majority this approach guarantees the slowest possible form of progress. Patience and intelligence create quick wits and flexibility. The expert player solves his problems before anyone else has realised that there are any.

Talent is mysterious. None of us knows what is inside us until we try to get it out. Practice must aim to release it, and involves learning new techniques, improving existing ones, and solving the daily problems presented by works being learned.

The solution of pressing daily problems is often the most bewildering to the student. The process of recognising which solution is the best and/or quickest is a matter of selecting the best option from the range available. I give a sample process in the Endnotes.

These methods need only one thing from the player: just 'Read and Do'. No verbal 'understanding' is necessary. The practice patterns themselves reveal all: they always flow from the simplest point of departure. They work by forcing the player to hear what needs doing.

> *The mastery of any one instrument, of course, is not the subject of this book. The subject is your mastery of yourself. Your genes are non-negotiable but the intensity of your work is yours only to decide.*
>
> *Do you want to be exceptional? Then you must make exceptional efforts in confronting yourself.*

Preparing for practice

- **Before the warm-up** a minute of controlled breathing – for performers on all instruments! – relaxes the body and clears the mind. It gives physical control and calmness to your mind and body, which, after all, is the instrument of performance. Follow that with one or two slow, catlike stretches.
- **The warm-up should be just that, and nothing more!** It is the preparation to play. Do not confuse it with real practice. It should be as short or long as you need for that limited purpose only.

- **Now take a break!** *Stop when the warm-up is complete. Take a short break of – say – 5 to 10 minutes, and then review the day's work ahead. This is vital in order to avoid drifting along aimlessly from one thing to another. Most of my own students have told me that this is the key to achieving a good day's work.*

Practising

Develop your own practice patterns.

The guidelines below are an aid to creating an effective way of working. I ask students when they begin their studies with me, to follow these guidelines for a month or two, so that the benefits of planning can be appreciated. After that they are free to continue with their own ways of working. Clear thinking makes for good practising. Muddled thinking means ineffective practising.

If you are just starting as a full-time student, you should practise in periods of up to 30 or 40 minutes, **and no more.** Then take a break of at least fifteen minutes. Do something quite different to refresh the mind. Stop before you want to: playing with poor concentration will send you backwards.

- Remember! Going on beyond your best attention span is damaging.
- Remember! You are trying to learn new things and to reform old bad habits. To achieve these objectives your concentration must be at a high all the time.
- Remember! Practice concentration is different to performance concentration. Keep freshening up by taking breaks.
- Spend a minimum of two hours per day on practice. Less than that is inadequate.
- Award yourself days off, regularly, at least once a week. The mind needs time to absorb and synthesise the work you have done, and the body needs time to become normal again!

Write down the elements to be worked on daily

For example:

            Pieces of music for performance

            Studies

            Technical work

            Scales and arpeggios

            Orchestral repertoire

            Sight reading

- Here is a suggested schedule – only a suggestion! – of four sessions, with the time in minutes. Repeat the sessions when you go beyond two hours or devise new ones. Make up your own.

- Keep the timings exact, because then you'll have a sense of working to a deadline, thinking fast and hard, rather than: 'What shall I do next? Can I stop now, maybe?' You'll be motivated by the need to work really well, because your attitude will be active, not passive. Stop precisely on time. In this way full attention is maintained.

- Continue like this for a definite period, say, four/six/eight weeks. Only then look back: you'll see its value, especially the improvement in consistency.

    Session One
    0 – 15   Technical work
    15 – 20   Bowing or Articulation exercises
    20 – 25   Scales and Arpeggios
    25 – 40   Pieces and Studies

    Session Two
    0 – 10   Technical work
    10 – 25   Pieces and Studies
    25 – 30   Technical work
    30 – 35   Sight reading
    35 – 40   Scales and Arpeggios

    Session Three
    0 – 10   Technical work
    10 – 25   Orchestral repertoire
    25 – 40   Pieces and Studies

    Session Four
    0 – 30   Pieces and Studies
    30 – 40   Sight reading

- Occasionally give yourself a day off and play for fun!

General points

At all costs avoid the 'patchwork' practice habit. That's when you start to play, only to stop at the first mistake or blemish. After some tinkering, you proceed to the next error, again stopping, tinkering, carrying on, and so on until the end. What have you done? You have not faced or solved any specific difficulties, and the technical issues thrown up by the difficulties have not been addressed either. Neither has the piece been performed complete and uninterrupted as it has to be in performance. No performing context has been established, even for a complete section. This is the worst possible strategy: you don't know where you are, except you feel as dissatisfied as before.

Try this method. When a work has been learned in outline, revise the difficult passages, then play it through as a performance. Play the difficult passages again, slowly, then put it away. Do not nag the instrument or yourself. If need be, re-think without the instrument, then put it away. Let your inner, hidden mind think about it without you interfering all the time!

Once thoroughly learned, play a work in long, complete passages. In these performances, ignore blemishes of any kind and do not respond in any way with annoyance, or any other childish tantrum. This will strengthen your performance attention and determination, and will focus you outwards on the work rather than inwards on your own over-sensitive ego. Then go back for efficiency practice of the passages that were unsafe. As I say many times, deal with 'the performance' on a different level to 'practice'.

Dealing with Studies. Technical studies are exercises abstracted from real-life musical situations. Their use is concerned with the physical demands made by the instrument. (Scales and Arpeggios, among the simplest and best of these, are undervalued and underused today.)

In any study, start from a different place each day and play in a circle to finish where you started. Studies are written as technical challenges, so use slow practice a great deal, and use your inner ear (your imagination) to auralise the difficult bars. Do not shadow finger or mimic playing: my experience is that it slows the learning process. After which, repeat, slowly if necessary. What does this do? It puts the mind in control.

Do not over-practise problems or new techniques. If you have a specific priority or problem for improvement – say – a certain type of articulation or bowing, each time a new timed practice segment starts, spend the first 30 seconds on that topic. 'Little and often' is the golden rule for improving technique; then put it out of your mind.

> *Is Failure a Choice?*
>
> *I have never taught a student who failed to become a professional player – IF – he was totally determined.*
>
> *Some players of greater talent have failed where some of lesser have succeeded. The latter chose success.*

Often a student will choose a priority topic and spend weeks highlighting it, hour after hour, day after day. The result is? Everything gets worse. The student often concludes in desperation that practice is bad for you. Wrong! His conclusion should be: **'Bad practice is bad for you!'** The capability of even moderate players is very complex, so what has happened? Answer – the normal balance of playing has been severely disturbed. All players know more or less where they stand in relation to their own capability, so when that balance is disturbed, trouble is the result. Unrealistic targets create despair by being impossible to fulfil. Obsessive concentration on just one aspect of playing wrecks the overall delicate playing balance.

It's all in the mind. The body can only do what the mind asks it. I will go so far as to suggest that virtuosity is a state of mind. Does virtuosity reside in daring to ask the question of oneself?

One at a time. With regard to technique, work at only one priority target at a time. Focus the mind on that alone. Holding many targets in the mind at the same time results in confusion in both practice and performance, and a sense of overload and stress. As in real life, if you or I try to do too many things at once, we quickly become confused.

I also underline that, at any one point, too much change creates uncertainty. By choosing only a single element of technique as the next priority, you and your teacher can be calm about dealing with it. Just as important, it allows re-adjustments to one's overall playing to happen without forcing. Humans work in an organic way – each element relates to and adjusts to all others in the system – each affects and is affected by the other. They need time to settle comfortably. As I have written several times in this book, little and often is the golden rule.

Finally, expect to repeat practice patterns over as many days as necessary. The most valuable practice aid is patience.

Question: What is the controller of co-ordination? Answer: The accuracy of your time-awareness. **Choosing the exact moment at which to play** is the co-ordinator for all the elements of technique. The difficulty of individual elements may vary enormously, according to particular demands of the notes being played, but the only common factor, that all the elements of playing must obey is the instant at which each note starts. For example, while the bow or tongue has an easy passage to play, the fingers may be struggling with awkward combinations for that passage, resulting in missed or blurred notes. When the player has mental control of time, the fog lifts from these problems and solutions are quickly found. The Time Pattern Exercises will show you whether you have accurate timing.

Aims, goals and making progress

Aims are general, but goals are specific. We all need aims in order to set sail at all, whereas goals are the landfalls, the destinations we hope to reach. The aspiration to succeed provides the map by which we can chart where we have come from, and where we hope to go. Allow yourself to dream to the limit – and then set about making it happen, step by step.

Check your progress over longer, rather than shorter time spans. Don't look back on a daily basis! If we look back day by day, the picture will always be confused, like a very jittery graph. Instead, compare today with three months, six months, a year ago. Then your image of progress will be realistic.

Only by taking a common-sense view of how we function – how we respond to the business of learning and the effect of positive and negative stress on that process – can we develop the capability to improve smoothly. When we try to master a problem by just uncritically playing it over again and again, we are being unintelligent and impatient – in a word, unrealistic – about the standard of our technique. We are also ignoring a fact of life, as well as musical life, that if a 'situation' isn't mastered quite quickly and smoothly, it will require serious work.

Expertise and know-how

I began this chapter by saying that practising works through expertise – know-how – in short, professional intelligence. Not the exam kind of intelligence, but quick-mindedness and savvy.

Firstly there is the knowledge base – the practical elements that allow us to get around our instrument – time, rhythm, pitch, dynamics, articulation etc. Most of the chapters of The Foreground section of this book cover these matters.

Secondly the more shadowy and abstract topics dealt with in The Foundation – such as Listening, Reading Music, Awareness, Memorisation and so on – when they are understood, they support the practical elements and help them to improve.

Thirdly, the technique of our own instrument is the area that most often, and almost always mistakenly, dominates our music-making.

Fourthly, above the others, the skills of Interpretation – the understanding of Music – bring our instrumental activity to artistic life. The musical picture, the artistic image, whether of a concerto, a phrase or a scale should be paramount in our calculations.

Fifthly, how to practise, how to perform, how to manage oneself as an individual, how to look after oneself, are all further areas of expertise.

The following chapters examine all of these distinct areas of knowledge, how to manipulate them, separately and together, in order to achieve the quickest progress.

3: Using the Elements ~ TURNING SOUND INTO TONE

Making the sound

Just before the moment of playing, hear and feel the sound that you will need for the music to be played. Watch any fine musician: you will see him prepare the moment of playing, addressing the instrument and the sound. All fine performers have a special absorption that is perfectly tuned to the task. Then keep that sound at the front of your mind while playing.

In my teaching I always start with an examination of the student's own sound quality as my first priority. The state of the student's playing is instantly revealed.

Sound into tone

Two or more notes form a context: creating a relationship between notes is the means by which the musician develops tone. Individual sounds become tone when they are linked together.

Tone varies in different musical contexts. There is no tone 'in general'. Nothing of value is ever 'in general'. Your 'individual' sound, and the way you vary it for the musical context, are what matters. Be careful not to produce what I call industrial musical noise – sound that it adequate but without life.

Whether you want to play expressively or brilliantly, **scherzando** or **molto cantabile,** will depend on the music in front of you. Whether warm, hard, brilliant, playful, sonorous – all tones that we create have to be imagined before they can be achieved. Remember! A musician is an actor with sound and phrasing, as opposed to stage actors who use word and gesture. Go through the imagination process a few seconds before playing: it will quickly become simultaneous with the start of the note. In the same way that boldness creates technique, so imagination creates sound, then tone.

The inner musical idea has to be constantly compared with the outer reality: the imagined tone has to be matched by the actual result. It can be a long, tiring process, but with patience it will develop. It is not an analytical activity but a listening, musical one

Your sound must be capable of variation in accordance with the needs of the music. The tone and the phrasing interact together to produce the illusion of expression, the thousand minute variations of time and tone that give character to performance – far too many ever to be described. Pianists, for example, often imagine specific orchestral instruments in order to achieve a mood. Alfred Brendel, the pianist, in **Musical Thoughts and Afterthoughts** has written down some of the methods and precise hand positions he uses to imitate certain instruments.

At one extreme – and the most natural – the singer's instrument is in the body. The sound that the voice makes is turned into tone by the singer. Tone exists in the way the sound is carried forward along the line of notes. At one remove, for those instruments that are breathed into or stroked, carrying the sound forward to the next note is still the essence of tone. The physicality of the relationship between sound and body is very close.

At the other extreme are the percussion instruments – the sound being created through an instrument that is separate from the body, among which we must include the piano. The physicality of hitting an intervening mechanism to create sound removes the player to some distance from the actual sound. Pianists, for example, like to distinguish between many types of touches and weights, and some will display untold contortions in their efforts to conjure a particular tone from their instrument. Unfortunately the laws of physics dictate that a piano key is quite unable to distinguish between being pressed down by a great pianist or prodded by the point of an umbrella.

So – you might ask – why are some pianists better than others? The reason lies in the relationships between the notes. Is there a musical, tonal shape to the horizontal progress of the sound through time i.e. the line? Is there an appropriate balance of the sounds in the vertical, i.e. the chord? These countless relationships, these artistic measurements, can only be controlled by your musical feeling – as it happens.

4: Using the Elements ~ CREATING THE MUSICAL LINE

The foundation of the line

Evenness of tone is the basis for creating a musical line. Subsequent shaping of the melody or melodic line we call 'phrasing', but, whether we are percussionists or pianists, wind players or singers, an underlying evenness of tone is essential. Where there is a **crescendo** or a **diminuendo**, or other such detail, the evenness of the progression must be comprehensible to the listener, in the same way that a sentence of words must be.

Aside from the sound quality that you are seeking, be sure that each note has the same volume. If a change of dynamic is in progress (a **diminuendo** for example), attend to the grading of the volume. Beware also of accidental tone and volume differences that occur when jumps in pitch are made.

Producing legato

To achieve good sound quality in **legato** (the binding together of notes) – as mentioned in the last chapter, firstly produce the sound, then carry it forward to the next note without interruption or distortion. Think of it as the same note moved to the next position even if it is to be articulated. This concept has relevance to pianists or percussionists even though the nature of their instruments is percussive: for them the illusion must still be created, but in other ways. Listen to how expert players do it.

Producing staccato

A musical line of disconnected notes needs continuity in exactly the same way: the relationship of succeeding tones must be unbroken. The only exception is where the composer deliberately dislocates the musical line by extreme contrasts.

Compare & contrast

Example 12 is a simple example of a couple of bars, playable by most musicians above beginner level. However there are enough variations in time values, and jumps in pitch, to allow an expert listener to differentiate easily between players. Play the example at a moderate **Allegro**.

Example 12

Now play the passage as a series of even-length **mezzoforte** notes as in *Example 13*, ensuring that they are of the same dynamic, shape and character. Do this several times, listening very carefully.

Example 13

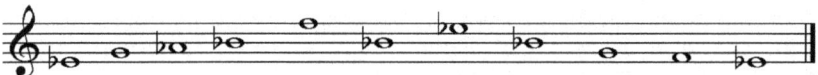

Finally play the original again. If you have achieved the required evenness of sound, the passage will be tonally improved, and – even for good players – the line will be presented much more expressively and clearly.

The next example shows how a musical passage can be worked to give an optimum quality of line.

Example 14: Brahms Violin Sonata in G major

Step 1

- Firstly, play as a series of separate long notes, as shown in *Example 15.*
- Now play slurred, in time, filling in the rests, as in *Example 16*. String players should use long bows.
- Repeat as many times as necessary, until absolute evenness is achieved.
- Listen again and again, even when the performance seems smooth. Keep matching it against your ideal of level, even sound. When the ear hears and the mind imagines well, the body will automatically adjust to produce the ideal. It does not need descriptions or analyses, it knows what to do – or will find out by trial and error.

Example 15

Example 16

Step 2

- Introduce more normal bow changes/articulation into the slurring. These should be as light as possible and be hardly audible as articulation. The even sound must be totally maintained; the effect is of an articulated slur. If spaces appear between the notes these will be accompanied by a slightly thin sound at the start of the next note, and then a mini crescendo as it swells to full value again – the 'twaa' effect. If the ear is careful in examining the exact points of change between notes, the arm, or the tongue will adjust to correct any loss of tone. With the bow, sustain the note to the last instant of time-value before changing direction. In the case of wind and brass instruments the tongue should come forward to the contact point as late as possible and leave as quickly as possible, thereby avoiding any break or distortion of the sound.

Step 3

- When you have achieved a fine **sostenuto** line, gradually introduce more normal bowings or tonguings into the phrase, inserting the rest. *A sense of continuity and evenness must remain in the playing, even when the music is not legato.*

Summary

This technique can be used for any passage, even very complex or very staccato ones. The principle of 'line' in sound production, whether the passage is **legato** or **staccato** or a combination, is one of the basics of good performance. The control of a note's shape is the control of its dynamic. The principle behind this approach is that of the **vocalise**, the singer's exercise that requires a melodic line to be sung on one vowel sound, completely **legato**. It cleans and purifies the musical line.

Remember

- These patterns may seem too much trouble, or much too easy to a player gifted with natural facility. My experience shows that players of every standard benefit from servicing and improving their listening in these ways.
- Remember! It is the ear and mind that we are training.
- Remember! The body can only ever follow the mind's instructions.

5: Using the Elements ~ MANIPULATING THE ELEMENTS

The three elements

The three elements of music – time, pitch and detailing (dynamics and articulation) – constantly interact with each other. These elements also intertwine with the workings of your technique. Do not therefore be surprised that problems occur: the complexity of these interactions creates many awkward difficulties. You must learn to understand these relationships – for example, which one is the dominant technical factor at any one moment – in order to guide your playing successfully. When the three elements are untangled, your ear discerns automatically the 'what' and the 'how' of providing solutions.

Examples 17 (a and b) in which the Elements of Time and Rhythm dominate.

Example 17 (A)

Example 17(B)

Example 18 in which the Pitch Element dominates

Example 19 where the Detailing Element (dynamics etc) dominates

My preferred method of curing technical problems is based on the action and interaction of the elements of music. In other words:

1. **Identify the order of importance of the elements, then**
2. **Set up a situation where the dominant element disciplines the others.**

Time example: see Example 17(b) above

In the case of a passage where timing and rhythm may be a problem,

- Play continuous quavers (eighths) on one note, to be sure that your timing is satisfactory.
- Play the rhythm on one note, i.e. subtracting pitch and detail from the passage, deleting the ties – although that is not a particular problem here.
- Add in the ties. Make sure that the timing and rhythm stay accurate, then add in the dynamics.

If a problem remains, then sing the rhythm, while clapping the pulse! (See the chapter on Vocalisation.) If necessary, reduce the *tempo* to a level where you become accurate, using a metronome to give the crotchets (quarters) as a guide.

Pitch example

When the movement of the pitches is awkward,

- Subtract rhythm and detail, and practise the sequence as evenly timed notes.
- Sing the awkward intervals till you know where they are going.
- Examine the pitches for intonation, especially how the context develops to imply harmony.

When a melodic line is giving trouble in terms of evenness and tone control, the simplest and best exercise is as follows:

- Subtract the elements that are irrelevant to the issue.
- Reduce the line to one or two adjacent notes, depending on the slurring ties that apply.

Once your listening becomes more discerning, benefits will immediately accrue to all parts of your playing.

Dynamic example

When quickly varying dynamic detail is difficult to handle, in competition with other difficulties – especially in the phrasing of some modern music – problems can be broken down into stages.

- On one note, test the range of dynamics you are going to use.
- Play the series of dynamics of a passage on one note, as a series of equal lengths, until mastered.

- Still on one note play the passage in rhythm, starting with slow rehearsal, if necessary.
- Without tempo, then play the pitches of the phrase with the dynamics.
- Finally, unite the three, starting with slow rehearsal, if necessary.

A change of dynamics can unbalance performance. Here are a few of the ways in which distortion can occur:

- Loud dynamics often distort technique. This most often has a knock-on effect on tempo, rhythm, detail. Accelerandi, in particular, can be difficult to achieve.
- Crescendi and diminuendi can also destabilise the elements.
- A soft dynamic can make articulation more uncertain. A phrase reduced to the rhythm on one note, can be heard clearly for un-evenness and related technical faults. What to do about the specific matter then becomes instantly clear.

6 : Using the Elements ~ LOOPS

What is a 'loop'?

A loop is a very short, enclosed passage, repeated over and over, in an exact *tempo*, whether at the correct speed or slower. As a practice technique, at first sight it may seem negligible. But, with the passage coming back time and time again, *in tempo* – without which it will not work – it is one of the quickest improvement methods that I know.

What does it do?

A loop is essentially for solving small problems. It shows up the **precise moment and location** of a problem. The cure is at once obvious, if not necessarily easy. You may say "But isn't the moment and location of any problem obvious anyway?" Strangely, not often! While playing, one's attention is often split between what is happening and what is about to happen. And if things have not gone well you may also be paying embarrassed attention to what has just happened!

How does it work?

Because there is no forward progression in a loop – it just goes round and round – a loop directs the player's concentration exactly and actively on the problem moment. In a loop there is only the 'now'. There is no continuation to worry about. The problem sticks out like a sore thumb. You have to listen! Guided by your ear and without any verbal explanation or interference, the necessary correction is obvious.

Using it

♦ To improve the musical shape of a short progression of notes, which then adds knowledge to your musical judgement.

Example 20a   b

- ♦ To clear up a time or rhythmic inaccuracy, which will add to your knowledge of your technique and co-ordination.

Example 21

Listen to any professional-level performer and you will hear well shaped detail and controlled technique. The finer the performer the better these will be, especially in the shaping of musical detail.

N.B. Each reader must select motives or short phrases from his own instrument's repertoire: every instrument has special corners that are tricky for it alone. Obviously the phrases (**examples 20 and 21**) given above may be awkward on one instrument but not another. Below I give examples from two of Beethoven's early Piano Sonatas.

Example 22 (Op 2 No 2, Scherzo – Allegretto)

Control of this figure is difficult to achieve in all of its versions. Best to perfect the first and then compare and contrast it to the others. The left hand versions of the phrase, and the variations in dynamics, all combine to complicate the consistent shaping of the figure.

Example 23 (Op 10 No 3)

N.B. This particular figure is ever-present in the last movement, in a wide variety of situations.

Summary

To cure a brief problem – a group of rhythmically tricky notes with a high difficulty content, or in a phrase that is awkward to shape in the time allowed – loop practice is invaluable. This practice pattern controls the player's attention – just like blinkers guide the horse – so that he is aware only of the timing and the shaping of the phrase. Attention sharpens into concentration. Once concentrated, the player's ear automatically experiments to correct the detail.

7: Alteration, Distortion & Simplification ~ SLURRINGS & THEIR USES

Underlying principles

Every player knows that co-ordinating the different elements of playing technique – fingering, bowing, breathing, embouchure etc. – is an ever-present concern. As I have written numerous times in this book, good timing co-ordinates these elements and gives the player control.

Using Slurring as a control

The curing of uneven passage work is achieved by the discipline of one physical action on another, rather than by purely musical elements. For example, applying different forms of slurrings to those written, improve the evenness of fingerings. An obvious example is in legato chromatic scales – often played carelessly and unevenly because they are thought to be easy – dividing the articulations into groups of six, four, three and two will immediately pay dividends.

This further simple example can be applied to any passage where smoothness and evenness are required. Further possibilities are shown in Chapters 12, 13, 14, on Scales & Arpeggios.

Example 24

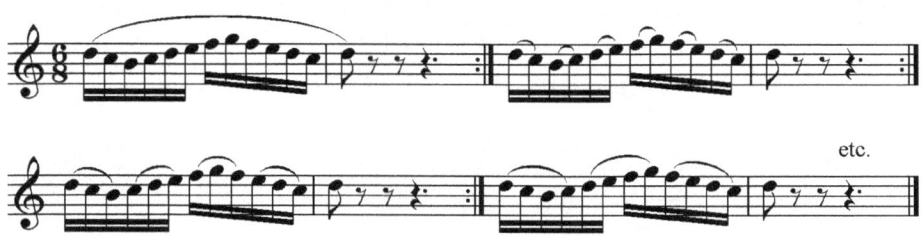

Experiment! Invent your own slurring variations!

8: Alteration, Distortion & Simplification ~ ALTERATION & DISTORTION

Tempo alteration

Slow practice

We all practise slowly when we are beginners. It allows us to learn unfamiliar actions and music, and begins the process that makes those actions automatic – if we continue long enough.

Slow repetition, as a start-up learning process, applies in most parts of life, education, training and sport. It remains arguably the most valuable practice technique we have, but is largely ignored once players pass the beginner stage.

Variable tempo practice

An adaptation of slow practice – variable tempo alteration – allows difficult moments to be worked on in context. Could varying the time become a bad habit? Quite the contrary! Deliberate application of *tempo* variation is utterly different to unconscious *tempo* variation. If you know what you are doing, you are in control.

The benefits of variable tempo practice

Everyone is familiar with the situation of practising difficult moments separately, correcting them, only to find that on putting them back into the context they go wrong again! This technique avoids that situation.

Variable tempo practice develops the player's ability to control his personal tempo within a performance. It also develops the player's ability to balance himself both as a problem approaches, and then while playing the problem. In performance a tempo can be varied by as much as 10% slower or faster – 20% overall – without the average listener noticing.

How does it work?

The ability to be mentally steady, while navigating difficult passages, is often the difference between the successful and the unsuccessful performer. This element of 'balance' refers to the expert player's sense of danger lurking ahead. For example, if, when out walking or running, you fall and hit the ground, the moment is painful and annoying, in the same way that an obvious error is to a performer. The cause of the fall, however, is what has gone before: the preceding loss of balance was the problem, not the moment you hit the ground. The same distinction applies to playing: a steady lead-in to a tricky problem and a controlled passage through it will produce surprisingly effective results.

All players respond differently to tension and crisis. If you rush when approaching a problem, disaster is likely. Variable tempo practice overcomes this unawareness: time and space become available – within any **tempo**. Many players find this technique very difficult to master, because it demands that the mind has an awareness separate to that being used in the actual playing. Some students have even told me that this practice technique hurts their brains!

Facing a problem passage

Let's assume that you know a piece reasonably well. You have practised the difficult moments slowly and responsibly – passages harder than any you have ever managed before, or passages where a variety of difficult challenges come one on top of the other – but there comes the moment when you decide to try it at full speed. At the critical moment chaos descends because of information overload. What should you do?

Solutions

- At the moment when clear thinking becomes difficult or impossible, introduce a short pause, a comma or a space, in order to allow yourself to regain mental balance. Then proceed. Within a few repetitions, you will be able to gradually shorten the pause or the comma until it can be dropped.
- Alternatively, introduce a **rallentando** just before the technical traffic becomes too heavy, negotiate the passage at a slower speed then accelerate out of it.

Of the four examples that follow, three become gradually more difficult, while the fourth is clearly much more difficult.

Example 25

Next?

Now go back over these examples and mark in the point by which you need to be looking ahead. (Musicians often use the symbol of a pair of spectacles for danger.) Then mark in a comma, a pause, a space or a ***rallentando*** that would allow continuity to be maintained while giving space to think. Rather hesitate than make a mistake.

So what was the problem?

In each case a technical or musical corner had to be turned. As a general rule, when there is a change of pattern or dynamic, there is a moment of greater or lesser instability according to the difficulty of the passage. If the adjustment is left to the actual moment – you are too late – you are left clearing up the muddle as you go along! You must be ready, in good time, to turn the corner. These techniques allow the player to proceed by managing the stress.

The problem can also be described as improving the player's speed of problem-solving – the speed of absorbing the situation, understanding it and then acting decisively. Think of the difference between the racing driver's speed of decision-making, compared to that of the normal driver's responses. A pro musician needs to be as smart as the first kind of driver: he's the pro.

9: Alteration, Distortion & Simplification ~ TARGET NOTES & ANCHOR NOTES

Target Notes

In broken passages – of mixed note-lengths and no particular technical patterns – certain notes are technically more important than others. If these notes are secure, the others around them tend to fall into place. I call these notes 'target notes'. They are often on strong beats, and – for those instruments whose high ranges are naturally insecure – are often at the high pitch points of a passage. In the rush to sort out problems it is easy to forget this solution.

Targeting these special notes must not become audible – 'thought' accents must not become obvious when the target note does not coincide with a strong beat or a phrase point.

Each family of instruments has its own characteristics and it is not the aim of this little book to offer any instrumentally specific advice. Choosing an example to illustrate this point would have no value, because the target notes probably exist at junction points where the technical problems posed by pitch, time and detail can be most conveniently brought together. Many solo musicians cover their scores with pencillings that add accents, lines or other emphases to help remind them of the best approach for that moment.

Anchor Notes

In running passages with notes of equal value, grouped regularly in threes, fours or more, problems often occur. Sometimes it may be unevenness of performace, or sometimes speed variations through a small part of the passage. Control can be gained by altering the values of notes.

With the first note of each group lengthened to be what I call an anchor note, the remainder of the group can be treated in two ways, for practice purposes.

1. The remainder can be quickened to maintain the original time signature.

2. The remainder stay at their original length, thus causing the time signature to be changed.

Without any doubt I find this technique the most valuable in conquering these kinds of problems. It can be varied without limit – including dotted rhythms for example – to be useful in many contexts.

The examples illustrate the principles involved. The Hungarian pianist Andor Foldes used the first illustration in his book on piano playing. It is worth saying that the whole piece, for those who don't know it, consists entirely of wide arpeggios in the same manner as the first two bars.

Example 26 (the first two bars of Chopin Etude Opus 10 Nr. 1)

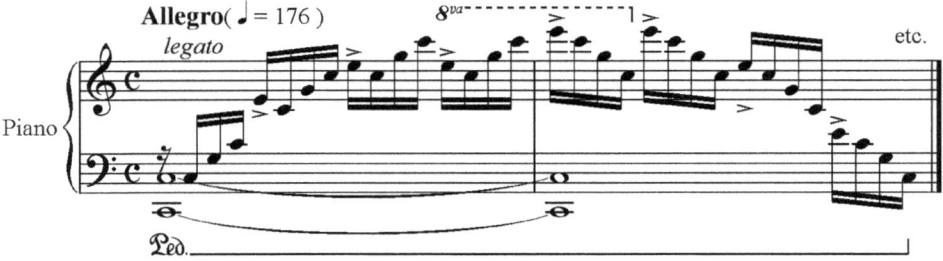

The speed of the exercise is determined by the player's stage of learning, while the quaver (the eighth) and the value of the shorter notes can be as long or short as suitable.

The distortion applied to the two bars given above read as follows:

> Not only was Chopin a composer of genius but obviously a teacher of equal talent. His two sets of Studies are (as are many of the keyboard works of Bach) wonderful examples of the two activities being combined.

Example 27

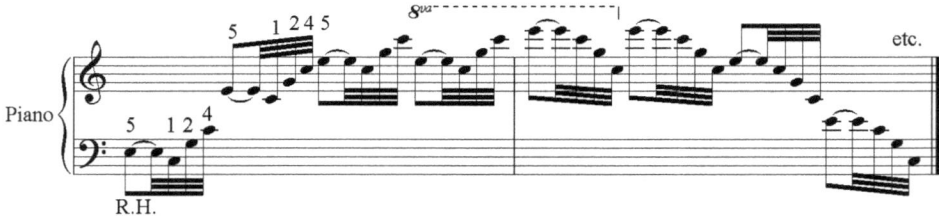

Take the following two bars from **Bach's Invention in A major** – the distortion can be applied to the whole piece as the figure is used throughout:

Example 28

Adjusted for practice purpose it looks as follows:

Example 29

Any run of notes – especially scales and arpeggios – can be re-formulated in many ways to enable control to be gained

Poise and composure

The best performers are notable for many things – balance under pressure is one of these. Watch any good sportsman or sportswoman and they are always like that. Performing composure is a skill: it can be developed through controlling the key moments of difficult passages. The techniques described above help to give that poise.

Footnote: Bach and Sons

Having mentioned Bach, the earliest example I know of this practice technique – that I discovered very recently during the final revision of this book – is in some study notes that Bach adds to Three Preludes from the **Klavierbüchlein** for his son **Wilhelm Friedemann**. In these exercises he recommends five types of distortion to use for study of the Preludes.

Example 30

10: Alteration, Distortion & Simplification ~ TRANSPOSITION

Why transpose?

Attempting a head-on confrontation with a tough problem rarely yields a quick solution. The mood created by such a situation is not appropriate for clear thought. Stand back. Think. If you want to go into the next room, do you take the shortest route, through the wall? No, you use the door, the corridor and then the next room's door!

Problems are almost always
1. *Solved quite quickly, or*
2. *Need very lengthy attention, involving new technical levels.*

Transposition allows a difficulty to be transferred to a 'comfort area' and then brought back, carrying the comfort with it.

How does transposition improve things?

Some passages persist in feeling awkward or remaining difficult, even after hard work. Whether the fault lies in a musical element – pitch, rhythm, dynamic – or in a technique – it still doesn't feel right.

Try the following: transpose the passage to a much friendlier register or key – say down or up an octave to begin with – gradually working back to the original through adjacent keys. The passage will change for the better because it has been through several perspectives. In addition, the lessening of technical stress in a friendlier key will allow the passage to be played more comfortably, because it is less intimidating.

Another value to transposing is that the player hears the phrase with a different sonority. For example, to hear a high phrase with an alto or tenor sound can be revealing of differing sound qualities that can perhaps be carried back to the original level. And vice-versa. Every new angle that is explored adds to your knowledge.

Example 31 (Mozart Violin Concerto in D, K218)

Even though the fingering is totally different, transposition allows the player to become familiar with the passage easily.

11 : Alteration, Distortion & Simplification ~ SIMPLIFICATION & ANALYSIS

Why simplify?

Be inventive solving problems. Simplification is just another way of looking at a problem. We all have experienced passages that contain a dark tangle of problems, where we know we are going to need a lot of high-wire luck to survive, even after much practice. Every new piece seems to have one or two of these.

How does it work?

It works by taking some of the heat out of the situation and allows your intelligence to get busy. Space is made around the problem, so that you have room to manoeuvre and to see exactly where the root difficulty lies. Simplification and rebuilding approaches a problem in a way that teaches by understanding and listening – in other words by self-education.

Simplification makes a phrase easier and offers an alternative route to mastering its difficulty. Change the timings, the range and the dynamics in order to give a fresh view of a passage, and to take off the pressure. As in sport, working towards a target does not mean tackling it head-on.

In the example below I have simplified the original before leading back to the real passage. The problem is dissolved gradually, in a series of steps.

Example 32 (Haydn Trumpet Concerto in Eb, 1st Mvt.)

This second example shows some of the possibilities of analysis in a different way, but in no particular step order. It is taken from the first movement of the **Beethoven Piano Sonata in Bb, Op.22.**

Example 33

> *Take the initiative. Create your own studies from the problems you meet. The activity will increase your general capability and make you more resourceful in looking for solutions.*

12: Alteration, Distortion & Simplification ~ SCALES & ARPEGGIOS

What are they?

Scales and Arpeggios are simplifications (abstracts) of what happens in real music. Used with imagination, they become mini-studies and introduce us to almost all the combinations of notes we are likely to meet in our playing career.

What is so good about them?

The daily practice of scales and arpeggios offers the fastest route to competence on any instrument. With very few exceptions I have found that the best players are very good at Scales & Arpeggios. Whether Scales & Arpeggios help to make a good player or whether a player can play them because he is good, whichever way round is irrelevant; they almost always go together.

For the moderate player, Scales & Arpeggios offer the best practical hope of steady and encouraging improvement. Not only do Scales & Arpeggios lead the player around the whole instrument, the very nature of the work instils regularity, discipline and method. The lack of these qualities in the first place is a probable reason for a player's mediocrity.

> *No one ever told me what Scales and Arpeggios were for, and what they could do for me. So I just did them when I was told. Now I know that they are pure gold. I use them – for myself – to this day!*

They are one of the prime methods of avoiding the day-to-day variability that musicians find so disturbing.

Yes, some performers have developed perfectly well without Scales & Arpeggios. It is not, however, an absolute rule. In their early playing life they must have done enough work of the right kind, and at the right time in their growth, to build up their playing intelligence and good habits. In these instances good luck allied to talent has produced an effective grounding. Thorough work on Scales & Arpeggios ensures that a good grounding is in place.

Creating fluency and confidence

Scales & Arpeggios create fluent, reliable knowledge of those patterns of notes that regularly appear in music. The same sequences of notes are constantly written and rewritten by composers in varying contexts. Scales deal with adjacent notes, while arpeggios generally deal with the non-adjacent. Importantly, arpeggios strengthen harmonic intelligence.

When automatic, this knowledge gives confidence to the player: you then know that almost all note-to-note relationships will have been mastered. If this work has been thorough, you can feel sure that your technique will stand up to the pressure of public performance.

Regard a Scale or an Arpeggio as a normal piece of music with an expressive character. It is as harmful to play one inexpressively as it is to play a valuable piece of music woodenly. Imagine it is by Mozart!

What do they do apart from annoy and bore?

Scales & Arpeggios guide you through all the nooks and crannies of your instrument, not just the well-trodden paths. Most players avoid certain keys and tend towards the easier – let's say the sunnier ones! The shady parts of an instrument's range, usually involving distant keys and awkward technique, are usually missed out in unplanned practice. Familiarity with the note-families that make up all the various keys gives added fluency to reading, sight-reading, and transposition. For those instrumentalists who have to read-and-transpose in orchestral performance – brass and occasionally woodwind – the dice are heavily loaded in favour of the player with a knowledge of Scale & Arpeggio patterns and therefore a feel for harmony.

Throughout this book I refer to the brain as a resource to be deliberately exercised and improved. Being no different to any other part of the body, the brain needs stimulation, challenge and matching work and effort. Without them it will not function well. Improve your mind, and your musical (and commercial) value will improve.

How Scales and Arpeggios help problem solving

Quickness of mind in problem-solving is an essential for all professional musicians, as is familiarity with the whole territory of the instrument. How many students remain uneasy outside the common main-line keys? The short but sharp challenges of Scales & Arpeggios give the player excellent training in problem solving and memory-recall under pressure.

The mental effort demanded by the study of S&A gives the brain serious exercise. Academic work in music has been all but abandoned in most schools, with the result that the ability to think fluently in music is dying. The effort involved in the study of S&A will go some way towards remedying this, by supplying experience of the basic interlocking maps of musical relationships. The passive use of the computer in school music is killing the acquisition of real knowledge: hoping that a computer will come up with something interesting in the early stages of knowledge is ridiculous.

Used imaginatively, with variations of musical style, rhythms, pitch patterns and dynamics, S & A, as mini studies, can be expanded to any size needed, and made relevant to any problem, for example, in a piece currently being studied. Being limited in duration, the player can give full attention to the brief task in hand.

Organising them painlessly

This is a sample method:

1. Write out the Scales & Arpeggios to be practised on individual slips of paper.
2. Take two jars or containers, then put the slips into one.
3. Draw out the slips one by one, and play the scale or arpeggio listed.
4. If played well, put into the second jar.
5. If not, mark with a cross and put aside.
6. In conclusion, practice the scales and arpeggios previously marked with crosses.
7. Put them back into the first jar.
8. Continue round and round, adding new slips on each circuit.

This method achieves random but consistent work on all Scales & Arpeggios. It ensures that you have a record of those Scales & Arpeggios of which you are uncertain. As you repeat this system, the weakest ones identify themselves by a growing number of crosses!

Practising them intelligently

Adopt a set routine when asked for a Scale or an Arpeggio.

1. **STOP!**
2. **THINK!** ... review it thoroughly – and only then
3. **PLAY!** ... *without stopping under any circumstances*. This ensures that you develop good recall of what is to be played and then a determination to see it through.

What usually happens is quite the opposite. **PLAY, STOP** at the first fumble, and then, too late, forced to **THINK**. A brainless anxiety results, with further false starts, and fingers hacking away in the hope of getting lucky. **STOP, THINK**, (that is, mentally recall and review until sure), then **PLAY**, is a routine which creates calm, steady playing which will be unflustered and will survive any superficial blemishes. The **THINK!** moment may be embarrassingly long to start with, but it will quickly decrease. This method also sets a pattern for any successful thinking under pressure, inside or outside music.

When you are not sure of a Scale or Arpeggio, mentally review the whole of it before playing, without shadow fingering – particularly avoid this habit when thinking through a scale. Just thinking the notes through results in faster learning. I assume that it is another example of the brain working best when doing one thing at a time, before attempting co-ordinations.

Achieve fluency without touching the instrument. The notes of all Scales & Arpeggios are best learned and revised without the instrument in hand. A great deal of valuable practice time and effort can be saved this way, and the ability to learn away from the instrument is strengthened.

The return leg of each Scale or Arpeggio is always more accident prone than the outward section. Remember to use deliberate variable speed playing, slowing into an awkward passage, and then quickening back to tempo once past. Perhaps add a pause at the top of a scale while reviewing the return leg: gradually shorten the pause as you gain speed of thinking. This will strengthen your control and balance when approaching dangerous passages.

I include examples of Scales & Arpeggios for use in daily practice in **Scales and Arpeggios: Examples** at the end of this section. While there are infinite variations possible, I show some that will test most players thoroughly. These examples offer advanced patterns and difficulty levels not found in the usual Scales & Arpeggios books. For the sake of space the examples given are all within a limited range.

At all times adopt a musical style. Treat each Scale & Arpeggio as a very short piece of music. There is no such thing as boring practice, only bored and boring players.

Further guidance

- When fluency has been achieved, start on a different degree of each Scale & Arpeggio each day.
- Often start at the top or thereabouts, as many difficult entries begin higher up in the range.
- Introduce different rhythms. See the examples.
- Go up on one Scale or Arpeggio, and down on another.
- Change on to another Scale or Arpeggio at each octave.
- Add extraneous notes, in ones, twos, etc. See the examples.
- Remembering that the turn at the top of a standard Scale or Arpeggio is the most dangerous part, and also that the return downwards is always more accident prone than the journey upwards, practise the top octave going up then complete the return to the bottom. Slow the Scale down – or stop – before descending, in order to prepared for the problems ahead. As competence develops quicken to normal.
- Practise in groups. Not only will this sharpen quickness of response, it will help you learn not to be thrown by others' mistakes – and your own – an essential skill for the professional performer. (Errors can spread like wildfire in an ensemble if players are easily rattled.)
- For a fuller listing of what can be done with Scales & Arpeggios, see the examples in the following chapter.

Remember! Repetition is the path to the mastery of any subject.

13: Alteration, Distortion & Simplification ~ SCALES & ARPEGGIO EXAMPLES

This set of examples – in C major and in two octaves – is given for illustration only, and is to be used in all keys, in major and both kinds of minor. It introduces some broken scales and arpeggios, but these are only a few of the endless possible variations. Also included are a few patterns for two players.

All scales and arpeggios should be mastered within a moderate compass, then extended onwards from there. Achieve fluency at each step before extending.

Example 34

Practice – Scale & Arpeggio Examples

Example 35

Practice – Scale & Arpeggio Examples

Example 36

Below are the five possible series of arpeggios in fourths. It is curious that this interval has been ignored in Scale & Arpeggio books and examinations. The fourth, both perfect and augmented, is as common in modern music as the third.

The starting note of G, and the two-octave arpeggio format, are chosen as a start-up illustration only. Once these are familiar, they can be transposed to all pitches.

Many other arpeggios are used in music – the augmented triads, for example, as are their cousins, the whole tone scales. Together with the diminished and dominant sevenths, one or more notes can be added to the major and minor triads to create arpeggios and scales of more than three notes. Every jazz musician has to know many of these variations just to get started with improvisation!

14 : Mind Skills ~ THE INNER EAR ~ AURALISATION

What is the inner ear? and Auralisation?

The inner ear is a figure of speech, a metaphor, for the power to imagine music in our minds: the rehearsing and performing of music in the imagination. Auralisation, the activity of imagining music, can be carried out at any time and in any place, with or without music.

What are the uses of the inner ear (Auralisation)?

- Firstly, *in interpretation*. Use auralisation to develop an overview of a work. Most musicians form their judgement of how to play a piece while learning the notes and simultaneously playing the instrument – a messy business. Become familiar with a work, develop a vision of it, and reflect on its structure – without the instrument. Once fluent in this type of mental rehearsal, the time for learning and understanding new pieces is cut radically.

- Secondly, *in phrasing*. Use auralisation to shape the detail of phrasings. With the instrument in hand it is likely that details are given an off-the-peg phrasing treatment, with safety as the priority. Without the instrument in the hand, solutions can be created from the music alone. You can imagine the daring option, and indulge in flights of musical and technical fancy.

- Thirdly, *in reading and learning music* – unfamiliarity with the notes, insecurity about 'what comes next' on the page – inhibits the process of playing. Isn't it obvious that when you come to play the instrument, the more you know of what comes next, the more positive your subsequent playing actions will be? Why? Once you know positively which note comes next, you can then give your instrument undivided, confident attention, freed from onfusion and uncertainty.

- Fourthly, *in technique*. Master mechanical patterns, such as Scales & Arpeggios, and the fingerings of difficult passages, by slow mental repetition. Interestingly a fingering problem-passage is best solved by thinking through the notes and their fingerings and not by constant replays. Furthermore do it **without shadow fingering on or off the instrument.** For some reason the miming of fingering slows down the learning process where it matters – in the mind. Think the fingering, but do not do it.

> A by-product of reading partially or wholly unknown works is that some players have the bad habit of peering forward at the music. Bad posture and cramped breathing result. String players, pianists and percussionists would be mistaken to think this is not relevant to them: poor breathing affects everyone's mood and physical efficiency.

Some general points

Talent exists in the unconscious: auralisation helps release the genie from that particular bottle. Without having to deal with the real life instrument, it is possible to dream freely of just how good you want to be.

We all have amounts of waste time, travelling, waiting for appointments and so on. Use this time for auralisation.

I sometimes ask my students to prepare a study or a piece for their next lesson, with the condition that the first time it is to be played is at the lesson. The results are generally extraordinary for a first effort, and on some occasions they could stand as a formal public performance. Before conducting, I do my preparation in the mind. I run critical passages through time and time again, constantly experimenting to achieve a convincing shape and flow.

The nineteenth century pianist Paderewski, who was an international soloist in the more leisurely days of train and boat travel, would often learn and memorise a new encore for his next concert – away from the keyboard – only playing it at the actual performance.

Sports scientists can find no physical differences between moderate athletes and those of Olympic standard. The only difference that can be identified in any way, shape or form is that the great athletes think about their event all the time, mentally rehearsing every element, time and time again. Likewise the musical performer who consistently thinks about style, technique and different ways to play will continue to improve, will develop as fast as possible, and will come as close as humanly possible to realising his talent fully.

Remember Liszt's dictum? If you have forgotten it – look it up again! (Practice – Chapter 2)

15: Mind Skills ~ THE INNER EYE ~ VISUALISATION

What is the inner eye? and Visualisation?

Visualisation is the act of seeing in the mind – visual imagination. In sports science it has long been established that the regular practice of visualisation is invaluable as a technique for growing potential. We anticipate, i.e. visualise events to come, sometimes with pleasure, sometimes not. Visualise in a conscious and controlled way in order to harness your faculty of anticipation. Like auralisation, visualisation can be carried out at any time and in any place, with or without music.

What are the uses of the inner eye (Visualisation)?

Performance, being very different to practice and rehearsal, must be mastered as a skill in addition to playing the instrument. The experienced performer has undergone thousands of professional performances and knows what to expect in almost any situation. Whether playing a solo recital in a small room, leading an orchestral section at a symphony concert, giving a masterclass, or recording a concerto, the expert player will have seen it all before. Visualisation short-cuts the lack of day-to-day experience.

Visualise the next performance you are going to give in public: repeated visualisations will supply some of the 'experience' factor. Visualise every move to be made on stage. Imagine as exactly as possible the hall in which you are to perform. Entering the platform, where you stand, what you do between pieces, how you treat and acknowledge fellow performers – your accompanist, for example. Look out from the platform into the hall from your playing position, whether standing or sitting. 'See' the audience and include as much detail as possible. Imagine playing into the space, and holding the audience's attention with your eyes, your presence and the sounds you are making. Feel the ambience of the place, the atmosphere and the acoustic, so that the sense of it is as realistic as possible. The more completely and often the experience is thought through, the more comfortable and normal it will seem.

Visualisation simulates in advance the experience of playing, helping to take the strangeness and uncertainty out of it. Once a player feels comfortable with an orchestra, an ensemble, or a hall, then performing becomes easier. The regular experience of playing in a particular place, or with the same ensemble, gradually makes the experience more familiar and therefore more comfortable. It is a natural animal response for anyone to feel uncertain in new situations.

For example, when you walk into a room containing total strangers you are very likely to feel watchful if not nervous for a few moments. A sense of insecurity is perfectly natural, but advance visualisations of situations help to make them 'ordinary'. Practise being nervous, then exercise the controls that you use to combat it: the unknown and frightening therefore becomes as familiar and normal as it ever can be. Expert performers never lose the heightened anticipation that precedes a concert, but they learn to use it.

All serious athletes use visualisation routines, seeing and thinking through their techniques, skills, and situations in order to make them automatic and familiar. Research has shown that intense visualisation as a learning process is only a fraction less efficient than actually doing the thing itself.

16: Mind Skills ~
THE INNER VOICE ~ VOCALISATION

What is the inner voice? and Vocalisation?

Vocalisation is – anything one does with the voice! *Lah-lah-ing, dah-de-dah-ing* – or shouting, screaming, laughing, crying – all these are vocalisations, just as singing or speaking is. The voice is our most natural instrument and, for this particular musical purpose, the less trained the better. Vocalisation can be a noise-shape rather than a sound – a vocal gesture without exact pitch. Whatever the quality of the sound, a positive vocalisation releases natural musical expression – but it must be full-blooded or it won't work.

What are the uses of Vocalisation?

When you feel musically 'stuck' about how to perform a phrasing or a rhythm, vocalise it (sing it) aloud in a totally uninhibited and unembarrassed manner. Vocalising will revive your positive musical response. Players who are 'stuck' almost always vocalise better than they play, which is obviously not the right way round! Anxiety often buries our artistry and musicality. Many a player worries about the instrument as if it were an enemy. The pain of past failures, and the fear of potential failures in the future, blot out everything else. Vocalising puts the player back in touch with his inner musicality and allows him to be freely expressive of the music's feeling.

Hands & voice

In exploring ways of releasing musical inhibitions, match some hand and arm gestures to your vocalisation. Watch singers: they use their hands and bodies naturally to bring out the expression of the music and to help find the response in themselves.

Mime

Try also using hand, arm and body gestures – mime – while vocalising something as ordinary as technical studies: at this more modest musical level you will still find graphic sound-shapes and gestures.

Music, after all, is the shape and gesture of pitch as it travels through time. Whether the gestures are vocal or physical, the actions tap directly into our senses. If you feel embarrassed by vocalising or gesturing, this is all the more reason to persevere with it. If you are as shy as that you have a problem! Kill your shyness before it ambushes your budding career.

Singing in Schools and Colleges -

In Britain now, singing has virtually disappeared from the education system. For student musicians of all instruments, regular singing has a uniquely beneficial and therapeutic effect, providing very valuable large-scale ensemble experience and an introduction to performing that never fails to thrill and excite.

Perhaps, most importantly, singing is educational in a true sense - the development of the whole person. I can remember at school some fifty (plus) years ago enjoying general music classes once a week that consisted of us twelve-year-olds singing concert and folk songs. <u>Everyone</u> read simple tonic solfa. Added to that, percussion bands were led by a teacher playing the piano - and so a solid groundwork was laid for playing an instrument a little later, with the rudiments in place and the appetite raring to go.

At the start of the twenty-first century, sixteen-year-old school students in Britain can now take the major national academic music exam without being able to read music!

17: Looking After Yourself ~ ANXIETY CONTROL

What is anxiety?

Anxiety is anticipation that has got out of control. We all experience anticipation, whether the event is musical, sporting, or of any other kind, private or public. It is a quite natural response: it alerts and sharpens our faculties. The downside, in regular high-risk anticipation, is that it can easily escalate into the habit of anxiety.

Uncontrolled anticipation quickens and tightens the breathing, which then interferes with all activities not just playing. This type of breathing locates high in the chest and pumps excess oxygen through the blood. It can lead to dizziness if taken to an extreme. When continuing for any length of time, it is accompanied by a sense of impending disaster and a lack of control.

What else causes anxiety?

Poor posture plus tiredness is another cause. Long hours of practice often create physical discomfort in the neck, shoulders and upper body, made worse by uncontrolled peering at music.

What are the effects of anxiety?

Apart from its obvious effects on the musician's performance under pressure, personality tests have revealed other negatives: anxiety destroys the sufferer's ability to notice the unexpected. In other words, awareness – of the environment in which the musician works and of his place in it – is destroyed. A kind of tunnel vision occurs that blots out reception of key performance clues.

Fear also blocks the retrieval of knowledge from the memory. We have all experienced the inability, under pressure, to recall material that we know very well.

Rigidity of the musculature is a common symptom in freezing of muscles caused by anxiety. The performer seeking to be a virtuoso is blocked: rigidity of the muscles and velocity never go together, as the pianist and teacher Josef Lhevinne wrote many years ago. If muscles are fighting each other they cannot be utilised fully for playing the instrument.

Controlling anxiety

Firstly, it is important to think of ***dissolving anxiety rather than confronting it***. The key disciplines concerning your aims and goals – of realism, patience and perseverance, together with sensible rest periods – are the foundations of an effective control of anxiety. Students often ask themselves 'Have I got enough talent to fulfil my hopes?' At music college level I have rarely found a lack of talent to be a problem, but the lack of a balanced approach very often is.

What are the build-ups to performance anxiety?

There are several scenarios. Anticipation builds to a pre-performance high, then transforms into extreme anxiety, and perhaps panic. Good habits seem to buckle, break, and the whole structure of playing crumbles in ruins. This state remains throughout the whole performance. Another scenario is that the performer experiences no significant pre-performance anxiety, but is suddenly hit by an explosion of panic during the performance, and a shattering loss of control.

These scenarios are in direct contrast to the controlled player who experiences anticipation, then a pre-performance high that relaxes when playing starts. This pattern of behaviour gives a definite lift to the performer.

Controlling anxiety in the short term

The most effective physical control for anxiety is good breathing. Breathing affects everything. It is the best measure of our inner state of mind, and is the most immediate route by which we can influence it.

Here are three exercises for daily use to help with the control of anxiety. Everyday use of them will give you a defence when anxiety threatens. Practical experience with students has shown that controlled breathing maintains stability, and prevents the onset of anxiety. However, do not expect these exercises to work if you adopt them as a last minute pick-me-up for a fast-approaching performance.

Exercise 1. Wall breathing

Preparation

Stand with your back to a wall. The head should lean back, full weight, against the wall. Shoulders should drop as far back and down as possible and then relax. Keep your bottom against the wall, but the feet can be a couple of inches away. Bend the knees slightly, so that the back is lengthened against the wall.

Action

Relax the front of the torso, top to bottom, breathe slowly and deeply. For most people this action produces a definite sense of relief, a sense of well-being and the lifting of anxiety. In order for this breathing to become constant, a one-minute spell every hour will create the habit very quickly. Soon you will only have to think of doing it to feel the relief!

Exercise 2. Field of vision eye exercise

Stare hard at an object two or three feet away. Note your breath pattern: in the vast majority of cases your breath will be high in the chest or stopped altogether when your vision is focused and staring. After a few moments, let your field of vision go peripheral, i.e. with no focal point. Be passively aware of the whole circle of your sight. Note your breath pattern again. When your vision is peripheral, the breath intake falls to the bottom of the lungs, to a position of relaxation and comfort.

Exercise 3. Calming movement

Stand with feet slightly apart, hands held in front of you at collarbone level, as if lightly holding a pair of reins, the fingertips loose, an inch apart. With unfocused vision, move the hands apart, extremely slowly and smoothly. This will slow your body's system down, reducing tension and easing your breathing. Use regularly, for no more than minute, perhaps during changes in practice.

Similar movements can be devised that give the same results. Those who find this type of movement beneficial, can investigate the methods of Tai-Chi.

Anxiety control on a performance day

Adopt a tempo that is slower than normal. Get up slowly, eat slowly, drive slowly, change slowly, warm up slowly, in fact, do everything more slowly. When you arrive at the moment to play, your total response will almost certainly be steady and unflustered. During my playing days, I simply noticed that it was what I did on those days, with highly consistent results. Anticipation becomes more enjoyable, and best of all, the performance can be savoured and is not over in a flash. You are in control.

Controlling anxiety long term

Control of body tempo is at the root of all these exercises. How we feel is controlled through our seeing and breathing. Good habits in these faculties give us control. If one has these good habits it is easy to say 'What's the problem?' For someone with bad habits, anxiety can seem like a maze enveloped in fog.

Staring hard, with the resulting breath tension, is the natural animal response to danger – this action gives superfast energy. It heightens our readiness to attack or defend as fast as possible, or to complete a task requiring intense attention (concentration), like threading a small needle. It is the normal response to an extreme situation. To be at that level of arousal permanently, which many people are, is a main source of anxiety and aggression.

Conclusion

In the long term, **the most important control of anxiety lies in the acceptance of our own fallibility**, which is why so many successful players say 'Just play! Don't think about it!' Of course you can't play without 'thinking', but worrying is the wrong kind of thinking.

The process is simple. Do your best, think over what you did, extract any lessons you can then forget it, throw it away as if you were crumpling it up like a piece of paper and throwing it in the bin! Start each day fresh, and while incorporating into your practice the lessons of yesterday, do it without guilt at having played badly, or undue satisfaction at having played well. Accept your errors, but don't resent them. They are as much part of you as your virtues. Even the expert professional player makes mistakes, but knows how to minimise them through experience.

The regular habit of drowning in shame at not playing well is pure self-indulgence, in the same way that shyness is egotistical behaviour. Even the finest performer cannot place an order with Saint Cecilia for a good performance. Accept yourself as you are. That way will ensure that your total response is balanced and increasingly reliable. Improvement will then come as quickly as is possible, even if not as quickly as you would like.

This process requires courage, because competition among musicians is quite pitiless. Only in sport, high-finance, business and the acting profession are performers discarded more ruthlessly. Ill-conceived aims and ambitions tend to rush young players onward too fast, often with negative results. There are also too many organisations who use young performers, especially singers, to fill roles for which they are not yet mature enough. The development process needs patience, persistence and realism.

Players who have become chronically anxious, often give the impression of being reluctant to let their anxiety go, as if it is a friend they don't want to leave, as if they will be totally naked and exposed without friendly anxiety! This is a state of mind that can only go on for so long before it is musically fatal.

Drugs for 'nerves'?

For years now drugs such as beta-blockers have been available on prescription. These suppress the flow of adrenalin created by anticipation. The physical symptoms of extreme anxiety, such as sickness, diarrhoea, trembling and panic are the result of an excess of adrenalin in the body. The well-known 'fight or flight' response is buried very deep in the primal parts of the brain.

I believe that there is clearly a negative side to beta-blocker use from the musical point of view. (I am not competent to comment on the medical.) The performance of a beta-blocker-user is almost always dull, which is the trade-off the player pays for a sense of comfort. The drug-user is also slower to respond to errors or emergencies. Expert performers can often sense a tricky moment about to happen, but this sense is not there in a drug user. The error occurs but is followed by an almost lazy recovery. Alertness, edge and sensitivity are absent: the comfort zone is an unexciting place to be.

It is standard practice to condemn the use of beta-blockers to ease performance anxiety. However, prescribed and used appropriately under medical supervision it would appear to be physically harmless, certainly in comparison to the amounts of alcohol, food, smoke and inactivity with which most people assault their bodies.

One string instrumentalist of my acquaintance used beta-blockers to counteract a bow trembling symptom, until one day, half way through a concert, he realised that he had forgotten to take the drug. He had not been nervous, obviously expecting the drug defence to be in place. The result was that the player was permanently released from the trembling symptom, and gave up using beta-blockers. Uncontrolled anticipation had been removed, even though by accident.

> *My preferred methods to give relief from uncontrolled anxiety would be, firstly, the one given under Control on a Performance Day. The second one is the habit of taking a break after warming up, in order to consider the day's work ahead. You can then learn to control and manage your personal tempo.*

18: Looking After Yourself ~ POSTURE

The value of good posture

Good posture enables. When posture is well-balanced, the body's musculature will do its work well, by itself. The body receives its instructions from the brain and enacts them with maximum efficiency unless impeded. Poor posture impedes and disables.

Quality of posture influences our breathing and therefore all our functioning including our playing. Posture controls the balance of the body, and influences health and mood.

Just because we are used to our prevailing posture does not mean that it is adequate. Habit is only that to which we are used. For example, many young people hold themselves tight in the neck and shoulders, resulting in permanently tender muscles and restricted breathing. Only in later life, when the body starts to complain loudly, do they come to realise it. Visits to chiropractors, homeopaths, acupuncturists *et al* soon – expensively – follow.

The section on **Anxiety Control** gives a series of simple checks for posture. Above all, good posture creates confidence. Confidence is a part of all successful activities. Look up, pretend to be confident, and suddenly you are! The world looks better through the middle of the eyes when the head is level. Watch the way people walk. If they look bright and confident that is almost certainly how they feel and operate.

Achieving it

In a precise activity such as playing an instrument, giving detailed instructions to parts of one's body to do this or that in order to achieve a specific result is fraught with danger. Unless overseen by an expert teacher, it will inevitably insert a new malfunction into the system. The inter-relationships among the body's groups of muscles cannot be controlled by trying to sense them as if they were separate from each other. There are too many and various interconnections –untold millions of them. Make one shift of tension or weight in the body, and it will be counterbalanced by a hidden responding tension elsewhere.

Violin and viola playing positions, in particular, are especially vulnerable. Not only is the playing position of the left hand and arm abnormal, it is held in a totally different manner to the right arm. The bodily asymmetry thus created fights natural human shape and balance. The cello – and other belly-out stringed instruments – uses the body in a much more symmetrical and therefore practical manner.

For brass players, breathing and embouchure are the two subjects most open to interference and abuse in this way. Every player has had the experience of pulling in here or pushing out there with the breathing, or stretching here or puckering there with the embouchure. Unless undertaken with an experienced teacher the result is always the same, a brief improvement and then a relapse into something slightly worse than before. Any interference in the form of deliberate, targeted tightening creates hidden tension. An extraordinary number of players hunch forwards in their seated posture, cramping the breathing system, the very basis of good posture.

> *It has become clear that lack of physical exercise, and the unnecessary and unnatural coddling of children that has become the fashion in the last twenty years or so, is already causing many young people in their late teens to be inadequately developed for long life. In former times, children would be encouraged to maintain an upright posture. A vigorous regime of physical exercise at school (and less built-in comfort at home), ensured a strength and stamina that was both physical and mental, and which are missing from the physical development of many of the present-day western world's young.*
>
> *Today, stress is exclusively spoken of as a negative force. The young child needs to experience challenges in an encouraging but disciplined setting, in the same way as it has a need for food and shelter. Good breathing based on good posture allows the personality to confront challenges without panic. I see stress as the energy created by challenges: our response can be either positive or negative. Response to challenge is one of nature's principal methods of testing and developing us, usually in some form of competition or contest with others.*

When we were babies...

Assuming that we are born free of defects, as babies we are in a near perfect condition. As a species we hover between being an all-fours creature and an upright one, but as we begin to sit in awkward chairs, sleep in unsuitable beds, suffer a string of accidents, small and large, we gradually lose our best posture and condition, and become crippled in small hidden ways. Watch a baby sitting, its back straight, relaxed but very strong.

Now we are old(er)...

A good upright posture, the head held high with shoulders relaxed, improves our whole mood. Modern research says that the body and the brain work best in this position, as opposed to the slouch. The bio-chemistry of the body is at its most efficient when posture is alert and bright.

19: Looking After Yourself ~ PHYSICAL CONDITIONING

What has physical conditioning to do with musicians?

The performing musician is a kind of athlete, using the body to create music. Playing an instrument is an athletic activity, requiring peak performance from parts of the brain as well as the appropriate muscle groups. Good physical condition, created by a sensible lifestyle, will improve energy levels that will in turn benefit the body's general health. The younger the age at which an appropriate routine is set the better. We need good food, moderate exercise, periods of rest from the instrument, and contrasting leisure activities.

Some people treat their bodies as if there were no tomorrow. When the body is youthful it can absorb a great deal of punishment, rarely complaining except for brief recovery periods. Changing bad eating, drinking and exercise habits when the body and mind are older, is very difficult indeed. Look around you! Any fantasy the human race has about being rational is disproved in the field of health alone! Homo sapiens? Obesity, for example, is almost always self-inflicted, caused by voluntary over-eating. Substance abuse may sometimes have deeper roots, but lack of exercise is voluntary.

> Could the youth but realise how soon they will become mere walking bundles of habits, they would give more heed to their conduct while in their plastic state.
>
> William James, The Principles of Psychology

Exercise

Choose a lifestyle that can be sustained. Over-elaborate systems of keeping fit are always quickly abandoned. Better to play golf, which is very popular with musicians, or to swim regularly, than to start an unrealistic routine. Walking is said by experts to be the best general form of exercise, and can often be incorporated into daily life without significant loss of time. Stretching is a natural form of animal preparation for action, and can be used without inconvenience. Fitness is not stored in a bank as if it were money. It is a battery that will hold for reasonable periods, but must be constantly recharged.

Binge exercising is distinctly dangerous to the body. As you get older your body will sharply remind you to respect it, with pulled muscles and other signals of disapproval. Occasional binge practising, the guilt of the unintelligent and the impatient, will also do nothing but cause trouble.

Diet

The alteration of eating habits requires self-discipline. For the purposes of common-sense living, a varied diet, which includes both food that is enjoyed and the good-for-you variety, is the most practical. Puritanical avoidance regimes –

the reverse side of binge-ing – put a strain on moods and feelings, which will then interfere with practising.

Quantity of food relative to exertion is also important. Excess of food is an overload to the digestive system. Beyond the point of need, food is a dangerous drug as much as any other. Our body is a once-only resource that cannot be traded in for a more up-to-date version once it has been trashed.

Our chosen instrument may be the hardware for our work, but ideally we should regard our whole person, mind and body, as the instrument. Treat it well. It is the only one you will ever have.

20: Looking After Yourself ~ HOW TO BE A GOOD STUDENT

Choosing a teacher

The student must answer the following questions.

- Can the teacher take me where I need to go?
- Is the teacher's approach the right one for me?
- Am I prepared to work hard and trust the teacher?

He should talk to the students of different teachers: it will become obvious from their responses, which of the teachers are effective and dedicated. The student must positively feel that the teacher will be on his side.

The student at college

A key mistake that can made by the student entering music college, or undertaking advanced study while still at school, is to automatically equate a well-known player's performing abilities with his teaching skills. They do not always go together. Master players can be totally 'natural', i.e. those whose thought processes are entirely hidden even from themselves, and who say that 'I just do it'. At the other extreme we find players who have an ability to describe what they do and have developed the craft of verbal communication.

Teaching is a skill quite separate from performing. A fine player will of course inspire by example. As a student this is how I chose my teacher. If they are also the 'natural' kind of player, analytical help may not be forthcoming when needed. Some teachers assume that what works for them, however individualistic, will also work for the student. This faulty logic assumes that the fundamentals of playing are perfectly displayed in their own work. I have come across the occasional player-teacher, whose rigid pronouncements have caused more problems than they solved.

When I once asked a violinist about the noted violin teacher Ivan Galamian, 'Was he a good player?,' I received the revealing response 'Oh no! he didn't play, he was a teacher!' Dorothy DeLay, at the Juillard School, only 'taught' the violin. During his cello classes Rostropovitch does not play: he stimulates by images and stories.

As I wrote in the Foreword, I present myself to my students not as a teacher, but as a remover of obstacles. Obviously this is playing with words, because I am able to guide with the benefit of a lifetime's experience. However, it clearly places the responsibility in open ground between the student and myself. The student has no doubt that he must teach himself, but also that he is going to get all the help I can give to him.

Keep a diary about your lessons – how you played, what were the comments made, how you responded. End with a summary of the experience. As importantly, go to concerts listen to music in general and not just the works that relate to your interests, and instrument. Do you want to limit your activity to being a musical bricklayer, or do you want to develop the ability to imagine and create on a wider basis?

Choosing to be a good student

The student's own input into the teacher/student relationship must be intelligent, honest and patient, otherwise very little progress will be made. So the next important question is 'Am I willing to work and respond to the teacher?' The answer to this question must be a resounding 'Yes!' otherwise the student should question his own career aims and ideas, before spending and probably wasting any more time and money. A teacher is a guide, and cannot program anyone and everyone to play well regardless of talent and application. Expecting the teacher to pour information into the student's mind, like water into a jug, is completely misguided. The student bears the responsibility to work along the path laid down by the teacher, even though the direction of that path may not at first be obvious.

All expert teachers have a vision of playing and performance, developed into a consistent whole over many years. For this vision to work best, the student must accept it completely, and should not treat the teacher's guidance as if it were an à-la-carte menu to be dipped into when it suits. The good teacher's view is created by experience, which is not available to a young person, however talented.

Practice and progress are the areas requiring the most thought and consideration. The organised student makes the least excuses, the fewest complaints and the best progress. When young players develop obsessions about particular aspects of their playing, an experienced teacher will offer guidance that will inevitably counsel a steady course of patient work. The unintelligent student 'wants it now,' at once, and goes about picking up a rag-bag of tips and hints from anyone who will talk to him. He then fritters his time away with hither-and-thither practice, in the hope of quick solutions, thereby destroying any chance of real progress.

The truth is that all musicians are, at root, self-taught. The good teacher helps the student to gradually take on responsibility for themselves in preparation for professional life.

What comes next?

Having done so much practice, with dreams of being a musician and hopes of a playing career, what are the choices that lie ahead? In music, our minds are free to enjoy some of the greatest thinking (in music) ever achieved by members of the human race, and we are free to rub shoulders with it, and with them. Yet for classical music the field is narrowing, as commercial pop and ambient music gradually fills all the available listening space.

Be alive to opportunities, don't wait for them to come to you. If you are alert enough, you will be standing in the right place when the big chance occurs.

Self-development versus standardisation

Below I briefly pose a few points for your consideration as you look ahead. You will not find these thoughts in any standard textbook, but to me they are as vital to your future as anything else I have written about.

The performing musician is a craftsman, and craft is at the opposite extreme to the mass production and standardisation that dominates modern life. Craft produces the unusual, the flexible, whereas standardisation produces the expected, the fixed. Anyone who is interested in the art of music, beyond the level of training for a job, must see life as a wide-ranging exploration fuelled by a self-education that never ends.

Education is the process of leading oneself outwards by study and self-improvement, as they merge with your life experiences and emotions. It is a random journey, almost always un-planned – and perhaps un-plannable. It is not for a fixed purpose and will sometimes take you to unexpected places, to fields that are not directly connected to music. But it will always feed back knowledge to your music and keep your mental life fresh.

> *Education is for the work of life.*
> *Job training is for the life of work.*
> *Quite a difference!*

The key fact about modern mass education is that it is standardised. The problem is that standardisation is not education: it job-trains people for work slots – but that is not education. It is anti-education. Standardised training produces standardised people. Standardisation in fact is the death of both education and creativity: square pegs into square holes is perfectly sensible when it comes to finding anonymous work-for-wages. The process of standardisation, with its gangster friend globalisation, will only be happy when cloning is the norm. But, by its very nature, classical music creation and performance cannot be anonymous. It is a process of continuous growth and change. It is simply a different animal.

What is the choice between free-flowing risk and standardised certainty? Risk offers stimulus, challenge, uncertainty, the chance of achievement and the very real possibility of failure. In a word, danger. Certainty offers predictability, routine and the absence of the possibility of failure. In a word, safety. You want both? Safe danger? It can't and doesn't exist. You can't have it.

A stimulating life awaits those who are alert to the unexpected and the random. That was my choice. Decide your own position for yourself. You choose.

Self-development and the computer

This innocent adding machine is the Trojan Horse in everyone's life. Like many other people, I use one almost every day. Where I draw my particular line is that I do not let it, ever, do any of my musical thinking for me. It is only a tool for helping with the housekeeping parts of my work.

Remember, it cannot be imaginative or compose for you, as the lazy-brained seem to think. It can only reproduce what someone else has put there. If relied on in the wrong ways, technology will strip your mind of its ability to be inventive and discerning, and will try to seduce you into thinking that you don't need all those tiresome academic skills. For musicians it is a mortal danger.

Remember, finally, that your mind will only develop by using it actively. If this little book prompts you to consider these matters then it will have been worth the significant trouble of writing it. Leaving aside family and friends, the only value you or I have to offer the world is what we know.

21 : Endnote 1

PERFORMANCE

There has to be a reason for all that practice. So I have added a chapter of simple guidance on performance.

Why is performance different to practice?

Performing is for the audience. It must be rehearsed in as many aspects as possible, because it requires a different form of attention and concentration to practising. Performance skill adds the essential public dimension to a player's work.

To perform is much more than just to play. Musicianship and technical capability by themselves are not enough.

The musician as performer

In the same way that an actor uses words, the musician uses musical sound. The ability to perform is quite separate from playing the instrument, or from musicianship. Many fine musicians will never be expert performers because they assume that musicianship and technique are enough. The performer must project a performance so that it captures the audience, whether of three or three thousand people. The most expert performers play with an audience like a cat plays with a mouse.

As in teaching, performance skill develops on a platform of rapport with the audience. Rapport gives the audience the sense that the performer is playing for it and not simply allowing it to listen as a group of outsiders. The performer must deliberately practise awareness of this contact, in order to perfect ways of performing and manipulating an audience.

The player who accounts for every detail when studying can then feel free to improvise when performing.

The audience-eye view of a performance

The audience is present to hear and to see the performer's interaction with the music. The public is fascinated to hear and see how performers work and deal with their task. Performers must remember that each member of the audience has made a substantial effort in order to go to a concert. A concert ticket, a programme, travel, food and drink are, taken together, very expensive. Having made the effort, the audience wishes to enjoy itself.

Therefore it is the duty of the performer to provide enjoyment in the best sense of the word. To come into contact with a personality expressing itself through musical performance is always a riveting experience for the audience. The relationship between player and listener cannot be taken to pieces and described. The performer creates it simply by wanting to communicate, in the same way that we are individually welcoming (or not) to another person.

Performance skills

1: Before playing, after playing and platform manners

A performance begins the moment the performer is first seen by the audience. Thereafter, until he disappears from view for the last time, all behaviour adds to or subtracts from the overall effect of the performance.

For a recital or concerto performance, the whole routine must be examined, re-examined, mentally run and re-run, time and time again, until it flows smoothly. (Visualisation.) Walking on, bowing, tuning up, the adoption of a settled manner of standing while not playing (e.g. control of fidgeting), the acknowledgement of applause, of the accompaniment, the walking off, with or without the accompanist, the return and re-acknowledgement of applause – these must all be appraised. When the routine can be envisioned seamlessly, the performer's total confidence rises and the last barriers between the performer and audience come down. Repetition is the key.

The natural performer communicates freely with an audience and needs only a little guidance. This skill can and should be learnt by all players. Each musician must create his own skill, because it is the individual personality that is being displayed to the public. I will describe how I try to develop it in students.

Firstly, the use of the eyes is critical in establishing that the hall is the performer's domain. The performance begins the moment the audience sees the performer appear from backstage. If the performer's eyes drag along the floor or are equivocal in any respect, the performer is at once weakened in relationship to the audience – which should be regarded by the performer not as many individuals but as one creature. The use of the eyes takes control; non-use of the eyes cedes control. The performer must 'own' the hall as his territory. Say 'Welcome!' to the audience with your eyes. And smile – at the least you will feel better for it.

As the performer walks on, his body language must also be convincing. A smooth but alert walk, timed, if possible, to match the size of the hall and the length of the audience's welcoming applause.

The use of the hands and arms can be an especial sign of unease. For example, if when talking to the audience the performer holds his hands in what I have heard called the crotch clutching position, the impression given is instantly defensive. Freedom of arm and hand movement is essential.

*A mistake, error or disaster must **never** be acknowledged or revealed to the audience. Always behave calmly even if you are internally engaged in a fight to the death. To do otherwise is un-professional.*

Any speech must be delivered a little more slowly, and with the voice slightly lower in pitch than normal. Care should be taken to keep enunciation clear and the vowels sustained. Breathy speech does not travel to the back of the hall. Phrase the sentences positively towards the key words, especially titles, composers and foreign words. Musicians especially should be professionally concerned with good pronunciation of foreign languages. The delivery of faulty pronunciation and the ensuing embarrassment demean the speaker.

The bow to the audience needs rehearsal until fluent. It is a matching response to the public's appreciation and should fit the scale of the room or hall and the type of performance being given. The large Romantic concerto suggests one thing, a small dry piece of modern music another. Once again – a smile is always appreciated in any circumstance!

2: During playing

Always direct the attention towards an imaginary audience. 'Play to the back of a large hall'. 'Project your music above the back row of the hall'. The limitation of the usual small practice room can easily stunt the musical personality, therefore the player should constantly have the audience present in his or her imagination. The command to 'Always play to someone other than yourself' directs the player's attention beyond the self and towards the outside world. Not only does this simple concept produce an attitude change, it also improves the musical and physical quality of the playing. It is one of the first things I say (when necessary) to a new student.

Thereafter a few supporting ideas help to develop the player's audience awareness. For example:

- If the music is being used, the stand must be placed in such a way that it is not a barrier between the player and the audience.
- If the music is being used, the player must give the impression that it is only being referred to and not read. Music being read too carefully imprisons the performer and prevents the essential contact with the audience.
- If the music is being used, at the start of a solo performance and until the first entry is well under way, the performer must keep his eyes on the audience. As in conversation, eye contact enhances intimacy and understanding. Eyes that are elsewhere suggest the person as a whole is not with you. Throughout the piece, each new significant entry after a *tutti* should start in the same way.
- Once this awareness is fully developed, our inherent ability to create relationships takes over. Each performer must use his or her native wit to develop the necessary contact skills. The initial impact of how the performer looks is crucial to making the best possible first impression with his playing.

3: Presence

The performer must appear comfortable. The audience, which watches as well as listens, will instantly assess the presence and mood of the performer. If the player appears ill at ease or otherwise uncomfortable, the audience will immediately sense it. Poise is close to stillness, while fidgeting is anxiety. Enjoyment is the whole purpose of the performance, therefore sensing discomfort in the performer spoils the experience.

Ease of presence whether real or apparent can be achieved by simple means. It also produces associated benefits for the player, in the same way as I outlined above in the example of playing to the back of a hall.

I suggest that the student performer does the following:

- Stand with the feet approximately eighteen inches apart.
- One foot should be a little in front of the other.
- The hip, knee and ankle joints should feel free and ready to flex and move.
- I then ask the student to move the weight sideways foot to foot, and also forward and backward. This allows quiet movement and positional change without moving the feet. This subtle mobility, or 'flow', suggests ease and comfort to the audience, which will relax, respond and be ready to react *with* the performer.

Preparation for a solo performance

All players give solo performances at some time or other. Everyone knows how tricky first experiences can be. Passages that seemed safe in the practice room go wrong, while some that were dangerous come off surprisingly well. Making the transition from this kind of pressured and unreliable playing to calm and secure performance needs very careful and solid preparation. The level of performance which master players produce, almost without fail, has to be earned over many concerts.

At some point all players who wish to become truly professional master players must undergo substantial periods of gruelling preparation for high-pressure events. The value of the lessons learned during these periods will be directly in proportion to the intensity of the preparations.

It is a revealing characteristic of the best players that they do not allow themselves to be fazed or thrown off balance by small blemishes, whether their own or other people's.

The degree recital

The degree recital, that comes at the end of college study, is a mini-Everest for all students. In spite of the many recitals or concerto performances they may have given along the way, the demands of this type of event are extreme. In many branches of education in Britain, such pistol-point examinations of ability have been abandoned as too cruel. Apart from the fact that, as in top sport, failure at music performance is a harsh and unforgiving experience, the value of the experience lies in its 'cruelty.' The performer's fear of failure is a spur that should be used to fire up his effort to improve.

- The programme should be finalised several months before the recital.
- The programme should be played through every day, on a five day-a-week basis. This play-through is quite separate from any other practice or work in hand.
- Ideally it should be preceded by a brief warm-up, and then a five minute gap before the play-through.

The play-through must be without stopping of any kind. The tutti rests are counted, and spaces are left between pieces as in the event itself. If the programme items are to be introduced by the soloist then this element should be included. Normal daily practice is quite separate to this play-through.

What is being done here? Performing is being practised. How rarely this happens! To travel this route of hard preparation is to make the journey from being amateur to being professional. Boredom is unintelligent and amateurish: the intensity and duration of the preparation matures the player musically and personally.

This process is to be carried out together with the visualisation as outlined in the paragraph on Platform Manners. Some weeks prior to the examination the student should take a couple of weeks completely free from the recital pieces, allowing the mind to freshen up.

> *The highest standards are gained very slowly, as layer upon layer of experience and know-how are earned. And the layers are sliced very fine indeed. The same principle applies to ensembles and orchestras as they are trained and built by those very few conductors who have the full range of skills necessary, skills that stretch far beyond the narrow confines of musical knowledge.*
>
> *The reverse is also visible as ensembles (and teams in sports activities) gradually decline. For the highest standards to be maintained someone must be doing the hard training work!*

After taking up the repertoire in the final days before the recital, the student and the teacher should accept the level of performance that has been reached. They have done the best they can. There should be no struggle to achieve last minute improvement.

The whole aim of this procedure is to mimic the event exactly as it happens on the day. The student will then be totally accustomed to the procedure, and will feel as comfortable as it is possible to be. It means, most importantly, that every conceivable sequence and combination of errors will have occurred and will have been survived.

Even if the student is not on top form come the recital day, the resilience given by this deep preparation will carry him through. The player's form will not drop below a certain level.

In the orchestra

When as a young player I first sat in an orchestra with some of the great players of the time, I immediately became aware that musically they commanded centre stage at the right moment. Their ability to frame a solo, to draw attention to it musically, added an electric charge and an aura to a performance that was indescribable, but totally unmistakable. All that is necessary for a performer to achieve this 'framing' is an awareness that it is possible and indeed necessary. When the performer has this awareness, it gives stature and magic to the playing.

Compare and contrast popular music performance

In popular music, where the performer's income derives directly from satisfied listeners, without subsidy, he has to fulfil the audience's needs or be discarded. In serious music, where most classically trained performers eventually hope to work, there is a distinct corruption of the relationship between performer and audience. Somehow because high art is thought of as a 'good thing' that needs no explanation – I happen to think that high art *is* among the greatest of 'good things', but it does need explanation and those in the arts should be able to explain why it is so valuable – many musicians give no attention at all to the audience as the focus of the performance. In the minds of many musicians the audience is negligible, a necessary evil.

This attitude results in poor concert manners on the part of many performers. Watch the behaviour of the average orchestra before a concert and during the applause! At the time of writing, attendance for most concerts is falling fast, and many former concert-goers are taking their free time elsewhere. The vigour and brio with which popular music addresses its audience is in marked contrast to the almost religious tone of much serious music presentation. In popular music, when the public loses interest, the performer meets instant obscurity. The musician who thinks of the public is unlikely ever to lack one.

22: Endnote 2

PRACTICE SUMMARY

Each day –

1. Form or reform the musical idea of the work or passage – the artistic image. Imagine it (auralise) and/or sing it (vocalise).
2. Play it through, or choose the method by which you are going to practise the harder passages.
3. Play, listen and repeat until satisfactory progress has been made or you decide on another practice technique. It may be that a longer-term strategy should be considered.
4. Review and decide what has been learned.

23: Endnote 3
PRACTICE CHECK LIST

MANAGING YOUR PRACTICE
- How to prepare for practice
- Develop your own practice patterns.
- Write down the elements to be worked on daily
- Avoid 'patchwork' practice
- Do not over-practise problems or new techniques
- Rest
- Controlling co-ordination
- Aims, Goals and Making Progress

MANIPULATING & USING THE ELEMENTS
- Sound & Tone
- The Musical Line
- Legato & Staccato
- Time ~ Pitch ~ Dynamics
- Loops
- Slurrings

ALTERATION, DISTORTION & SIMPLIFICATION
- Tempo alteration
- Slow practice
- Variable tempo practice
- Target Notes & Anchor Notes
- Transposition
- Simplification and Analysis
- Scales & Arpeggios

MIND SKILLS
- The inner ear – auralisation
- The inner eye – visualisation
- The inner voice – vocalisation
- Mime

Finally, a short unofficial CODA ... an informal mini auto-biog by your author in the hope that it may whet your appetite for a life in music ...

I studied trumpet, piano, harmony and counterpoint at the Royal Academy of Music in London. This was after a childhood playing in brass bands but with no tuition apart from the rudiments, and finally, just before the end of my schooldays, studying the piano for a couple of years with a very good teacher. My schooling, starting during the Second World War, was a very broken-up affair due to a variety of family circumstances: I attended 11 different schools between the ages of 5 and 16.

I entered the Royal Academy of Music around my 17th birthday, studied for three years, gained no qualifications except an LRAM (Performers) Diploma ... degrees were not on offer in those days, still not long after WW II had ended ... and left to pursue a career as a professional trumpet player. In June 1956 I was still 19 and had no idea what lay ahead. I started my career as an unknown freelance trumpet player, which culminated in the post of Principal Trumpet in the London Symphony Orchestra. While in the LSO I recorded as a soloist and appeared in concertos twice on BBC1 TV. I was also Chairman of the Board of Directors of the Orchestra for 5 years. As was common at the time, I also enjoyed a busy freelance career alongside my LSO duties, playing in the London studios for many films and other varied sessions where I had the pleasure to get to know players from all over the musical spectrum, not just on my own instrument or in my own discipline. I revelled in the astonishing range of expertise that still exists to this day at the highest levels of London performers, and have never tired of learning through working with these colleagues.

Leaving playing in order to conduct was a relatively easy decision particularly with the support of my wife: I wanted new challenges. I founded the Wren Orchestra, initially as a chamber group, but subsequently regularly expanding it to symphonic status, giving hundreds of concerts and broadcasts with Capital Radio over two decades in the London area. Orchestral recordings of a wide range of repertoire date from this period, from Mozart and Haydn, to Tschaikovsky, to Gershwin and Copland. I have conducted, amongst others, the Royal Philharmonic Orchestra, the Philharmonia, the City of London Sinfonia, the London Mozart Players, the Ulster Orchestra, the LSO Brass at the Barbican and the former Philip Jones Brass Ensemble at festivals and in recordings. Particularly satisfying was a period as Musical Director of the English Haydn Festival, a composer I particularly value.

All the while wishing to maintain my roots in the brass world, I included conducting brass bands alongside my orchestral conducting, but also arranging and composing, mostly but not exclusively for brass instruments. As a brass band conductor, I initially brought Desford Band to prominence: again an extraordinary learning experience in how to train and develop an ensemble. This was followed by the rebuilding of Foden's Band, a very different experience ... every group has its own culture ... but even more valuable. Later the development of the Eikanger Bjorsvik Band in Norway constituted yet another new experience, dealing with not only a new group but a different national culture.

Two 'firsts' of mine, that give me cause to smile even today, were unconventional then but are completely accepted now. Firstly, while I was the Musical Director at Desford I introduced female players into top-rank brass banding. For me this was not a matter of positive discrimination, simply that the best player, regardless of sex, should be appointed to a vacant position. Today women are everywhere in music, on merit, and nobody gives it a second thought. Secondly, while working with Desford and Foden's, to my surprise I came to be regarded as one of the brass world's more 'interesting' arrangers, so much so that I founded a publishing company, Rakeway Music, in order to satisfy a steadily increasing demand for my works, both in the brass band and the orchestral communities. As with 'women-in-bands,' traditionalists regarded my approach to arranging and scoring as 'dangerous,' even 'toxic,' as if I were hacking away at the very foundations of banding, especially in my advanced use of bizarre percussion and mutes for all band instruments! (The good old days indeed.) In effect, I backed into publishing by accident and certainly not by design. Today this form of publishing is common, not only in brass bands but in wind bands also.

I began teaching while still Principal Trumpet with the London Symphony Orchestra, but when I stopped playing I continued my teaching activities (eventually trumpet, conducting, and the writing of music) alongside my conducting activities. An 18-year period at the Royal Northern College of Music, a large portion of which was as part-time Head of Brass, saw the Department's reputation rise to rival any in the UK. The 1980s and 90s at the RNCM were non-stop times of innovation and fresh ideas for me, a magic roundabout of projects whose aim was to stimulate the Brass School. I started the Brass Band Course which continues to flourish to this day. I instituted Celebrity Brass recitals and lectures. I ran two large-scale Brass Conferences. For 3 years, with Foden's Band, I promoted the first ever regular series of original brass band music concerts in the UK. It was all great fun. One result of my teaching experiences was my book 'The Trumpet – Its Practice and Performance, A Guide for Students,' which was very warmly received on its publication in 1997. 'The Art of Practice' followed a few years later, written for student performers of all instruments. In 1998 I moved on to fresh pastures and an appointment as Professor of Trumpet at the Royal Academy of Music in London, which continued until my retirement from teaching in 2011. I still particularly prize my election as a Fellow of the Royal Academy in 2001, in addition to being an Associate.

I and my wife Angela live in retirement in South Western France, but I still work, although it is now centred around composition and home, with just the occasional foray into conducting. You will have gathered correctly that I am not an academic person at all: I am as far from that as possible. I am a 'doing' person. Everything I have learned has come in one way only: from doing, then thinking about it, then doing again. If this brief informal sketch gives some idea of one musician's journey traveled, beware: you will need a temperament that enjoys risk. The world in which I began my career has now totally gone, but new, as yet unimagined opportunities lie in wait for those who seek a varied and fascinating musical life. Just aim high. Higher!

The very best of luck!
Howard Snell - February 2015
Website, with catalogues of music, at
www.rakewaymusic.co.uk
Blog, on music, music people, anything and everything, at
https://howardsnell.wordpress.com/

www.ingramcontent.com/pod-product-compliance
Lightning Source LLC
Chambersburg PA
CBHW070453090426
42735CB00012B/2539